Turning Points 2

More Defining Moments that Shaped the Character of Top Business Leaders

Randy Schuster

Turning Points 2

Published by Indaba Press

Indaba, Inc.

Saint Petersburg, FL 33710

727-327-8777

www.Indaba1.com

www.RandySchuster.com

ISBN – 978-1-58570-017-7

Printed in the United States of America.

RANDY SCHUSTER

More defining moments that shpaed the character of Top Business Leaders.

Table of Contents

RANDY SCHUSTER

More defining moments that shpaed the character of Top Business Leaders.

RANDY SCHUSTER

More defining moments that shpaed the character of Top Business Leaders.

Foreword

You can do anything you want in life as long as you have the heart and the passion to do it

The above quote was my inspiration for the first **Turning Points** book, a project designed to showcase some of the many success stories that we have here in Rochester. It was successful beyond my wildest dreams.

More than 2,000 kids in the Hillside Work Scholarship Connection (HWSC) program were connected with the book, and through the generosity of Danny Wegman more than 6,000 copies were donated to 19 of the Rochester City High Schools. The city schools created a curriculum out of the text, and the book sparked as essay contest. You can read some of the winning essays and stories at the Turning Points website, www.RandySchuster.com.

Each essay is a testimony to the drive and potential of Rochester's student population, and it is a treasure to me to see how the book resonated with them. Students wrote

RANDY SCHUSTER

More defining moments that shpaed the character of Top Business Leaders.

about their dreams of owning their own clothing stores, restaurants, and service businesses. They talked about how the humble beginnings of many of the individuals featured in the first **Turning Points** book reflected their own situations, and how they were inspired by those from every background who had overcome illnesses, doubt, poverty, and setbacks to become leaders and winners. Many also marveled that all these successful people were proud to call Rochester home, and seemed intrigued that ties to Rochester may have been a part of what helped each one thrive and succeed.

Along with their marveling and admiring, the students who read the book are very focused on the nuts and bolts of being successful. Their essays reflect a realization that hard work and determination are essential for thriving in a competitive world. They point to the stories and acknowledge that they will face adversity, setback, struggles, and stress in pursuing their dreams. They are not afraid - but they do have more questions.

After the publication of the first book, my publisher and I started to receive questions from students who wanted to hear more about not just the life lessons but also the money lessons. There are many books available talking about money to teens, but most have a technical orientation or

RANDY SCHUSTER

More defining moments that shpaed the character of Top Business Leaders.

a focus on stocks and bonds. They lack the philosophical integration between living life and earning money, and an infusion of the life experiences that make money lessons real to younger readers.

The aim of this book is to again share the life lessons of some of Rochester's most successful business people and community leaders including a focus on money lessons. You will read about people who started with nothing but were inspired and motivated to build their own businesses as well as those who came into family businesses, put their mark on the operations, and took things to a whole new level. Through it all, you will get an insider's view into the defining moments and money lessons of these high achievers, and learn how those lessons have helped them accumulate wealth and build up their businesses.

Like the first book, **Turning Points 2** is designed for you to be able to pick it up and read a story or two whenever you have a spare moment. Read it over time, and whenever you need inspiration.

It's my hope that young adults - or readers of any age - can learn and implement some of the lessons on these pages so that they can go on to become Rochester's next business leaders.

RANDY SCHUSTER

More defining moments that shpaed the character of Top Business Leaders.

Confucius said "**A journey of 1,000 miles begins with a single step.**" A journey to a lifetime of success can begin with the inspiration of a single page.

Enjoy reading,

Randy Schuster

RANDY SCHUSTER

More defining moments that shpaed the character of Top Business Leaders.

iv

Dedication

Turning Points 2 would not have been possible without the support of many different people, all of whom deserve my sincerest thanks.

To my wife, Erni Schuster, my endless thanks for being my best friend and the one I can always turn to for support. Your patience enables me to realize all of my dreams, and none of this would be possible without you.

To my wonderful sons, Danny and Matt Schuster, who continue to grow and turn into young adults, taking responsibility, taking initiative, and creating passion of their own. It's a joy to watch your journey. Danny, you have grown so much since you have gone to college, and are truly showing that there are no limits to what you can do in life. Matt, you continue to mature in your high school years and I look forward to watching you take off over the next four years as you head out to college.

To my office manager, Delia Costanzo, who is a hub of the

RANDY SCHUSTER

More defining moments that shpaed the character of Top Business Leaders.

v

operations, tying everything together. Marie Eizenarms, my thanks for staying disciplined in our process and coming up with creative solutions. To Sharon Rollins whose passion and work ethic I truly appreciate and who keeps the appointments on track. To Kris Dussmann for the versatility and guidance you provide, and to Crista Deniz, for the supporting role that you play along with Kris. To Jim Cerone, for all of your support and ability to allow me to continue focus. To Hellen Davis, who I have learned so much from and will forever be grateful. To Julie-Ann Amos and Helen Ford for all your assistance with the editing for this project.

And yet with all these thanks, how could I overlook the roles of the 33 people who donated their time, energy, and life stories to this book? None of this would have happened without your support and the truly inspiring ways in which you have lived. On behalf of myself and all the future readers of this series of books, my deepest thanks.

RANDY SCHUSTER

More defining moments that shpaed the character of Top Business Leaders.

Introduction:
Al Simone

President Emeritus Rochester Institute of
Technology 1992 – 2007

---

*"The impala wakes up in the morning
knowing it must run or else it will get eaten
by the lion. The lion wakes up in the morning
knowing it must run or else it will go hungry.
The moral: It doesn't matter if you are an
impala or a lion, you have to run."*

African Parable

WHEN I WAS APPROACHED BY RANDY SCHUSTER TO TALK
ABOUT MY LIFE STORY AS AN INTRODUCTION TO THIS
BOOK, I COULDN'T HELP BUT REFLECT ON THE FACT THAT
EACH PERSON FOLLOWS A PATH. FOR SOME THAT PATH IS
LINEAR, WITH A CLEAR BEGINNING AND END. FOR OTHERS,
THE PATH IS WINDING. THERE ARE DETOURS, OBSTACLES,
AND OPPORTUNITIES. YOU MAY NOT ALWAYS BE ABLE TO

RANDY SCHUSTER

More defining moments that shpaed the character of Top Business Leaders.

vii

SEE THE FOREST THROUGH THE TREES, BUT YOU ALWAYS END UP SOMEWHERE.

That somewhere isn't always where you expect, and the harsh reality is life isn't always fair. Instead, a life story is a journey over time, and during that time you have experiences and meet people - have turning points, if you will - that shape who you become. It's up to you how you respond to them and what you do with them.

In my case, the path from where I started to where I am now has certainly been full of twists, turns, obstacles, and opportunities. Through it all I credit my parents for helping make me who I am today. They gave me the chance to live two lives from a very young age, and their influence stays with me even now.

My mother and father grew up in the North End of Boston. It's the Italian section, and mine was a second generation immigrant family. My parents grew up kiddy corner from each other and they were poor, living with shared bathrooms, coal stoves, and ice boxes instead of refrigerators. Just as I would, they started working long hours at a young age. My father worked in his family business, while my mother took a job working in an upscale ladies clothing store, and that

RANDY SCHUSTER

More defining moments that shpaed the character of Top Business Leaders.

viii

job changed my life.

It wasn't the money - it was the chance for her to see a life outside of the North End. From her experiences at the shop, my mother made it very clear to my father that when they were married they were going to move, which is how we came to live away from the rest of the family in Somerville, and later Winchester, Massachusetts.

Still, it wasn't like I was separated from the family. Every Saturday and Sunday until I was 15 years old I would visit the North End to see my grandparents and the rest of my clan. It was like I had two lives at that time - a Monday to Friday life with my parents in a green suburban haven full of professionals and white collar folks, and then Saturday and Sunday I was back in the land of the blue collar. On the weekend, I played "baseball" with a rubber ball and broken broom stick handle on cobblestone streets. During the week, I played with a real ball and bat on grass fields. These two lives were invaluable in helping me learn to interact with people from all walks of life.

I was very interested in sports, especially baseball, and in the business side of life. My father worked reselling farm containers with his father. The main action took place on

RANDY SCHUSTER

More defining moments that shpaed the character of Top Business Leaders.

the waterfront in Boston, and working in the business was a hard day's work. From the time I was 10, I used to join my father in his routine on the weekends and in the summer - up at 4:00 a.m., leave the house at 4:30 a.m., be at the docks by 5:00 a.m. and work until it was dark. My father did that his whole life, and I remember he never missed a day of work. I credit my work ethic to his influence, and also my ability to get back up and keep going after a setback.

Even though my family was from the North End, I was viewed as an outsider by the waterfront bullies, and had to learn to deal with them from a young age. It was great training for handling would-be intimidators later in life. I also learned to deal with people, and to treat people the way you want to be treated.

One day near the end of high school I told my dad I didn't want to waste time going to college. He almost had a fit!" Do you want to do what I do the rest of your life?" he said, challenging me. I realized that if I didn't continue my education, I really would end up on the docks forever.

I enrolled at Tufts University and earned my undergraduate degree in economics and mathematics.

RANDY SCHUSTER

More defining moments that shpaed the character of Top Business Leaders.

My years at Tufts hold many fond memories for me, not least of which because it was there that I met my wife, Carolie. It was a blind date neither of us wanted to go on, yet we haven't seen anyone else since. She's my best friend and the love of my life, and she's put up with me through all the other steps in my path.

Earning my Ph.D. at MIT was a beautiful but very busy time in my life. Part of the issue was finances. I paid my own way through college and grad school, and I did it by working. Not working just a little, either. I was my father's son and I knew about hard work and how you needed to hustle for a buck. I had some scholarships, but I still had to live.

At first, I worked for my father, loading and unloading at the docks. When I wanted a job on the assembly line at the Ford Motor Company, **I started asking them in September for a position starting the following May. I think they thought I was a little nuts, but I visited them every two weeks, and sure enough, in May they sent me a note to show up for work.**

When I hit graduate school, I mixed the hard work I was used to with the start of my teaching career. I would unload freight cars for A&P from 6:00 a.m. to 5:00 p.m., and then I

RANDY SCHUSTER

More defining moments that shpaed the character of Top Business Leaders.

taught a class at Northeastern University on Tuesdays and Thursdays from 7:00 to 9:00 p.m. It was another case of two lives - a union job on one hand, and an academic's life on the other.

Eventually I dropped the freight job in favor of teaching 22 hours a week for Boston University, MIT, Tufts, and Northeastern. I ended up writing my own textbooks for the courses, and getting into consulting. This helped my income, as I got book royalties, consulting fees, and my teaching salary.

I worked doing all kinds of things. When I accepted a job with the College of Business at the University of Cincinnati, I formed my own company, Quantitative Analysis Incorporated, and did work for Procter & Gamble, Cincinnati Milacron and Kroger Foods. The work was great and I loved combining it with teaching, but academia had another surprise in store for me.

I loved people, helping get things done, and making things better. When I was a faculty member, I decided that if I could be a department head I could make things better for me and all the other professors, so I became a department head. Then I thought if I could be Dean, I could make it better for

RANDY SCHUSTER

More defining moments that shpaed the character of Top Business Leaders.

xii

me and all the other department heads. Then I got to be a Dean, and it was fun, and I thought if I could be a President or a Provost, then I could make it better for all the deans and the whole university.

It became a challenge I couldn't resist, though I still think of myself as a faculty member who does administration. It's just another chapter in my two-sided life, really, and it launched another turn in the path. I took a position as President of the University of Hawaii, traveling Asia and building wonderful connections on behalf of the faculty there. It was a great time for my family and a great experience, and contributed to the path that brought me here to Rochester as President of RIT.

MONEY LESSON

Along the way I've learned that giving back makes you feel good, and you can give both money and time to make a difference. I like to say, **"Everyone can be rich by lending a helping hand to someone else."** Obviously, material wealth matters, but don't expect to get anything out of life you didn't earn. Save before you spend, and be sure to set aside a portion of your income for education and personal and professional development.

RANDY SCHUSTER

More defining moments that shpaed the character of Top Business Leaders.

Once you've met your own basic needs, cultivate an attitude of thankfulness and remember all of those that don't have your advantages. Look for ways that you can give of your time and your resources to help the less fortunate. Contributing to the happiness and success of another will help you in your own life and serve as a payback for the generosity and assistance you get from the world.

The pages ahead are full of stories of people who've worked hard and have found a way to share their wealth and good fortune with the world, even if it is just through the words of their stories. Whether your life is a two-sided journey like mine, a curved road, or a straight path to success, those behind the publication of this book and I hope that you will find inspiration and guidance in these pages.

All the best,

Al Simone

RANDY SCHUSTER

More defining moments that shpaed the character of Top Business Leaders.

xiv

Lynn Allinger

President of Craft Company No. 6

"The Power of a Dream-Passion, Creativity, and Imagination."

Dan Clark

THOUGH SOME THOUGHT SHE WAS CRAZY AT TIMES, LYNN ALLINGER HAS BEEN LOYAL TO HER CHILDHOOD PASSION FOR CREATIVITY AND CRAFTS. NOW A SUCCESSFUL BUSINESS OWNER IN THE CRAFTS INDUSTRY, HER PATH WAS NOT NECESSARILY A SMOOTH JOURNEY. HARD WORK, SACRIFICE, AND A WILLINGNESS TO FOLLOW HER HEART MADE IT ALL POSSIBLE.

Lynn grew up on Long Island as part of a blue-collar family. Her academic career was mixed from the start, as her true passion was for projects, creating things, and fashion. She would start her day with, "What can I make today?" even though her teachers and parents were less than impressed with her attitude.

RANDY SCHUSTER

More defining moments that shpaed the character of Top Business Leaders.

Still, Lynn was thriving in her own way. She knew that she couldn't depend on her parents to fund her every craft or fashion desire, so she started making her own things at a young age. Her original dream was that she would make it to Manhattan to work in the fashion industry.

A report card full of mixed A's and D's didn't bode well for her college prospects, but her parents were insistent that she go to school, and Lynn wanted to get away from Long Island. Her guidance counselor told her mother, "Lynn is not college material - she should just get married and have babies." Lynn found it funny, but still worried as to whether she would be accepted given her academic record. She'd targeted Oneonta State, which was as far from Long Island as she could get based on her parent's guidelines.

Oneonta did accept her and pushed by her parents, Lynn enrolled in the education program. However, after only a year she knew teaching was not for her. She switched into the major closest to her passion - then called home economics - maintaining her erratic study performance but deeply enjoying her college experience.

After college, Lynn found life pulling her to Rochester. Instead of Manhattan's fashion scene, she took a job with

RANDY SCHUSTER

More defining moments that shpaed the character of Top Business Leaders.

2

L'eggs Hosiery. The company was just getting started, and working as a salesperson felt a lot like running her own company. Looking back, Lynn feels it was an ideal entry for her into the business world, but in the six years she spent with L'eggs she also pursued her own crafts interests on the side.

Her sister had joined her in Rochester, and together they worked on several side businesses. One involved rebuilding and refinishing antique furniture. To improve her skills, Lynn enrolled in a night woodworking class at RIT.

Lynn's woodworking class would prove to be pivotal in a number of ways. Not only did she learn new skills, but the instructor was Gary Stam, a man who would eventually become her life partner and husband. However, first he would be her business partner. Together they founded Exotic Wood Designs, the forerunner to Craft Company.

It was a very busy time for both of them. Gary worked as an instructor at RIT, and Lynn maintained her job with L'eggs. Nights, weekends, holidays - every spare minute was spent with the business. Their first wholesale trade show appearance in the mid-1970s was so successful they were almost overwhelmed.

RANDY SCHUSTER

More defining moments that shpaed the character of Top Business Leaders.

The business was running on a shoestring as it grew. **"We had one pitiful old van, we didn't go out for dinner, there were no new clothes - all the money we had went into the business,"** she recalls. The woodshop was located in the basement of her house, and as the income from the business picked up, first Lynn and then Gary quit their other jobs. She wasn't concerned about losing the income from her L'eggs job because the more time she had for the business, the more money she could make there.

As the business grew, she and Gary considered renting more space, but friends advised them to keep their expenses low and stay out of debt, advice that the couple took to heart. **"It was difficult,"** Lynn recalls, reflecting on the state of the house in busy times and the challenges of keeping up as the business got bigger and bigger. She began taking her work to the national level, selling to stores like the future Craft Company around the country.

Even at this point of success, Lynn wanted more. She wanted to have her own gallery and store. One day out biking with Gary, they came across an old firehouse. It was love at first sight for a rough warehouse structure with brick walls and a paved floor. Stopping to talk with the owner, the couple discovered the building was for sale. Would they really like to buy it?

RANDY SCHUSTER

More defining moments that shpaed the character of Top Business Leaders.

Laughing now, Lynn recalls that buying the firehouse - now the home of Craft Company No. 6 - was when her friends really thought she'd gone crazy. It was 1979, and they'd paid $110,000 for an old building in a rough neighborhood. **"We loved it and thought we could make it work."**

Gary went to work renovating the interior, and the first thing they did was open the front room as a gallery. The woodshop left Lynn's basement for the back of the store, and using a small line of credit from their credit cards they bought merchandise for the craft store. It was the early 1980s, and interest rates were sky-high. No bank would touch a pair of crafters, so they had to rely on themselves to make things work.

In 1983, opportunity came knocking. It was Architecture 83, a forerunner of HomeaRama. Lynn and her business were involved through the Rochester Art Dealers Association to help decorate the interior of one of the homes. At the last minute, the furniture supplier pulled out. The architect was desperate. Lynn saw the opportunity and said, "I'll get the furniture."

She turned to her connections at RIT and the network of crafters in the Rochester area that she had built. Together, they filled the house with phenomenal handmade furniture

RANDY SCHUSTER

More defining moments that shpaed the character of Top Business Leaders.

items. The project was a hit - people took notice, and suddenly Craft Company was on the map.

As the business grew dramatically in response to the exposure, Lynn realized that she needed to know more about running a retail business. She joined the National Retailers Association, and focused on educating herself about business. **"For many artists, there's the attitude that money is not their forte,"** she notes, but she was able to attend seminars and learn what she needed to know to manage the company.

Along with building her business acumen, Lynn was also actively engaged in networking. It was a challenge initially, but she made herself attend luncheons, seminars, and business events until she felt like she was part of a community of successful Rochester women. Many of those she met she considers to have been mentors, inspirations, and valued advisors.

She became a part of the Rochester Women's Network, the local chapter of the National Association of Women Business Owners, and was a trustee of the American Craft Council, a national organization. Each group provided her with supporters, advocates -- and customers! She

RANDY SCHUSTER

More defining moments that shpaed the character of Top Business Leaders.

vividly remembers giving a presentation and having one of the group members standing up and praising the shop. **"Networking has been so important for both me and the business. It is very important,"** she says.

With increased community connections, business prowess, and a higher public profile, Lynn's Craft Company was on a steady upward path. Twists in the industry - such as the arrival of the Internet - offered opportunities and challenges. Lynn recalls taking an entire winter to learn how to manage the company's website, so that she could more completely express the company's personality on the web. Yet embracing technology has been just one piece of planning the future for Craft Company. Lynn sees a bright future for the company and the partnerships that she has built, with a lot of potential down the road.

MONEY LESSON

Looking back on her journey with a financial perspective in mind, Lynn is glad she had a strong work ethic and ambition from a young age. **"If I wanted it, I had to do it myself."** At times, her family didn't always understand her desire to continually have more - her mother in particular looked at her ambition to get what she wanted as a negative trait. However, Lynn views it as a positive, noting that it has carried

RANDY SCHUSTER

More defining moments that shpaed the character of Top Business Leaders.

her through a lot of tight times and penny pinching to get her business up and running just the way she wanted. **"We were always stretched for money and it was very difficult,"** she recalls, but by keeping expenses down and persisting even when others thought she was being crazy, Lynn has been able to create a successful company built around her passion for the crafts industry.

RANDY SCHUSTER

More defining moments that shpaed the character of Top Business Leaders.

Joe Bucci

Vice Chairman of American Rock Salt, LLC

"One of the best ways to cultivate a possibility mind set is to prompt yourself to dream one size bigger than you normally do. Let's face it, most people dream too small, they don't think big enough."

John Maxwell

A MINE FLOOD AND A BUSINESS CLOSING COULD SPELL THE END FOR MOST PEOPLE . . . BUT FOR JOE BUCCI, IT WAS JUST THE RIGHT OPPORTUNITY. A LIFETIME OF HARD WORK COMBINED WITH BEING IN THE RIGHT PLACE AT THE RIGHT TIME RESULTED IN A COMPELLING OPPORTUNITY FOR JOE. WHAT INITIALLY WAS PERCEIVED AS A DISASTER TURNED INTO A PROSPEROUS BUSINESS FOR A MAN WHO BELIEVED IN EDUCATION, HARD WORK AND DRIVE.

Retsof, NY in the 1940s and 1950s was hardly a cosmopolitan area. The town, about 45 minutes south of Rochester, was

RANDY SCHUSTER

More defining moments that shpaed the character of Top Business Leaders.

9

anchored around the local salt mine, and all of the 99 houses there were company owned. The population of just over 1,000 people was 80 to 85 percent Italian, most of them immigrants who had arrived looking for a better life in America.

Joe's family had followed that same path. His grandfather came over from southern Italy to drive a mule and run muck salt for the Sterling Salt Company. His father, a promising York Central High School grad, passed on college because the family didn't have the money for tuition, but came out of his military service to work his way up at the mine until he was chief engineer.

Looking back, Joe feels that his childhood was very unique. As a small, close-knit community, Retsof was a safe and open playground for kids. You could wander the four dirt and gravel streets freely, surrounded by houses that never locked their doors, and be looked after by every Italian grandmother on the block. Friends from grade school were friends for life, and sons followed in their father's footsteps straight to a job in the mines.

In its own way it was a great place to live, but Joe never thought he belonged in the mining business, even though

RANDY SCHUSTER

More defining moments that shpaed the character of Top Business Leaders.

he had worked part-time in the mines like most local boys. His path was college thanks to football. At York Central High School, his grades suffered while he focused on his game, but it seemed to be paying off. The first game of his senior year, 10 college scouts - including one from then powerhouse Syracuse - came to watch him run for five touchdowns and a win.

The second game of his senior year was also filled with college scouts, each of whom witnessed a running player's nightmare; a broken ankle. Suddenly, Joe's football dreams were transformed, as he was no longer a hot property. Frustrated and depressed, Joe was still committed to using football to become the first kid in his family to get a college education. With his injury and his grades, his options were limited, but the University of Tampa offered him a chance that he gladly took.

Joe's two years at the University of Tampa were transformational for him. He was officially there to play football, but as things played out he had only brief moments of glory interspersed with heavy doses of bench time. With football no longer at the center of his life, Joe focused on school and began to really do well. He got his grades up, became a solid B student, and used his new GPA to transfer to SUNY Geneseo.

RANDY SCHUSTER

More defining moments that shpaed the character of Top Business Leaders.

In a bit of irony considering his early academic performance, Joe was studying to be a history teacher. There was a serious demand for teachers at the time, and he had nine job offers and one phone call waiting for him after graduation. The phone call came from York Central, asking if he wanted to come back to his alma mater to teach history and help coach the football team. He readily accepted the York offer.

It was a bit odd walking the halls at York again, considering that his same teachers were still there and many of the kids he taught were the younger brothers and sisters of his own classmates. Still, there was no doubt that Retsof was home in ways other communities never could be. Joe married his college sweetheart from Geneseo, Elaine, a Rochester native and a teacher herself, and threw himself into his work.

Joe loved teaching history, noting that even now if he had his choice he would be sitting with a history book, reading for hours. There was just one problem - his salary. He started at $5,200 a year and he knew he had to do something else with his life to earn a living.

In those days it was relatively straightforward to get a real estate broker's license, so Joe got his at the tender age of 22. His father helped him get an office near the school, and

RANDY SCHUSTER

More defining moments that shpaed the character of Top Business Leaders.

12

Joe threw himself into a double life. He taught school from 7:30 a.m. until 1:00 p.m., and then worked at his real estate business until seven or eight o'clock every night and through the weekends. It was an intense schedule, but nothing that Joe wasn't used to doing.

Joe had always worked. He'd worked in the company store in high school, tended bar at the Cartwright Inn and put in long hours at the local mine. **"From a young age, I never stopped thinking about being successful and making a lot of money. That is why I constantly worked hard,"** he recalls. One Christmas break coming back from Tampa, he went to work in the mine before the sun was up, and didn't quit until after sunset. He laughs that he only saw the sun on Christmas Day and when he got on the plane back to Tampa.

That intense work ethic came in handy as Joe juggled the real estate business with teaching for the next 15 years. He built up a tremendous appraisal business and partnered with the mine to buy and sell mineral rights. He continued to work with the mine even after his father was killed in a mining accident in 1975, sticking with them as they transitioned from being the International Salt Company to the Dutch-owned AkzoNobel.

RANDY SCHUSTER

More defining moments that shpaed the character of Top Business Leaders.

In 1997, the Retsof salt mine, which had been operating since 1920, flooded and collapsed. The mine was inoperable, but the Dutch committed to rebuilding. They spent $18 million working to restore the site, and then one night Joe got a call from the plant manager that chilled his bones. "I just got word from overseas. The Dutch said they are not going to build a new mine." The next day, Joe stood with the management team in front of the 400 mine employees as the news was made public.

For the first time in his life, Joe saw guys he went to high school with crying. His students, his friends, fathers, sons - Retsof's generations were rocked to their core. Joe looked out at the misery and realized that the future of his hometown was at stake. "I've gotta do something about this."

A week went by. Two weeks. Joe had a conversation with a local banker, that led him to Gunther Buerman, an attorney in Rochester, and Neil Cohen, a financier from New York. They arranged to buy the mine from the Dutch for $3 million, and subsequently rebuilt the mine themselves.

Today, American Rock Salt has 306 employees, 48 of them former students of Joe's or his wife's at York Central. The

RANDY SCHUSTER

More defining moments that shpaed the character of Top Business Leaders.

annual payroll is $19 million, and four million tons of salt come out of the mine each year. It's the second largest producing salt mine in the world, risen up like a phoenix from the shattered mine that came before it.

Joe is thrilled by the success of American Rock Salt, and deeply enjoys working in the mining business. Though he never thought it was for him as a child, now he can't imagine giving it up. **"I like coming to work every day,"** he says. Along with managing the mine, he is active on community boards and spends time with his children and grandchildren across the country. Through it all, Joe relishes life in the town that has always been his home - Retsof, whose dirt streets have truly given birth to a rare opportunity.

MONEY LESSON

Joe considers a strong work ethic and a solid education to be the foundational elements of financial success. **"I have always told my boys that if you work hard and get your education, things will happen in life and you will be very successful financially."**

Joe has always conveyed to both his students and his sons to never demonize the pursuit of wealth. **"There's nothing wrong with wanting to make a lot of money, because then**

RANDY SCHUSTER

More defining moments that shpaed the character of Top Business Leaders.

you can do a lot of things and follow your dreams." Some of the things Joe has been able to do include buying a home in Florida, building a horse farm, donating money to SUNY Geneseo, and starting his own charitable foundation. He laughs that he has given more money back to York Central than he ever made there as a teacher, and enjoys giving back in quiet ways, too. He looks forward to the opportunity to do even more for Retsof and his favorite causes in the years ahead.

RANDY SCHUSTER

More defining moments that shpaed the character of Top Business Leaders.

16

Ann Burr

President of Northeast Region for Frontier
Communications

---

*"The future belongs to those who believe in
the beauty of their dreams."*

Eleanor Roosevelt

ANN BURR HAS HAD MANY OPPORTUNITIES IN LIFE TO SAY NO
AND TURN AWAY FROM CHALLENGES. HER COMMITMENT
TO SAYING YES, TAKING RISKS, AND EXPLORING AREAS
OUTSIDE HER COMFORT ZONE HAVE CREATED MULTIPLE
TURNING POINTS IN HER LIFE. AS A RESULT, SHE HAS BEEN
ABLE TO CONTINUALLY BUILD ON HER EXPERIENCES TO
CREATE BALANCE AND SUCCESS IN LIFE.

As a child, Burr was supported and inspired by her parents.
Her mother provided her with a creative, right-brained
inspiration, while Burr credits her father, who is a member
of the National Collegiate Tennis Hall of Fame and still on
record as the "Winningest Coach" in tennis history, with

RANDY SCHUSTER

More defining moments that shpaed the character of Top Business Leaders.

giving her highly competitive genes.

Burr is also very thankful to her father for ensuring that she received a college education. **"My degree was a strong foundation that enabled me to open doors that might not have opened otherwise."** She went to Utah State, her father's alma mater, earning an education degree and planning to become a teacher.

Fate had other plans. When Burr graduated in the late 1960s, there was a glut of secondary teachers on the market. As a result, she had no choice but to seek out a job in the business sector. Rather than being a depressing choice, it proved to be a key turning point in her life. Burr liked the business world so much that she made it her career.

Newly married, Burr joined Mountain Bell Telephone. This presented her with her first taste of the telephone business. After the birth of her first child, the family moved to Honolulu. Burr looked to rejoin the telephone industry at the local firm, Hawaiian Telephone, but found a better fit in the emerging nascent cable industry.

Oceanic Cable based in Honolulu was a growing company when Burr walked through the door. **"It really was the early**

RANDY SCHUSTER

More defining moments that shpaed the character of Top Business Leaders.

days of cable television, so I had the opportunity to grow with the industry," Burr notes. She ultimately spent 13 years in Honolulu with Oceanic.

She remembers many wonderful opportunities coming her way as she moved up the ranks at Oceanic. It was a smaller company, but growing very rapidly. Unlike many legacy telephony companies, promotions were based on merit and proven ability rather than seniority. Burr felt that the environment at Oceanic provided her with the opportunity to be a pioneer and grow right along with the cable industry to be successful professionally.

The pioneering and trail-blazing environment at Oceanic offered Burr an endless series of opportunities to grow and develop as she rose from Operations Manager to Vice President of Operations. In those days, the full package of cable channels and cable capabilities was still being built. Burr's location in Honolulu had her surrounded by inventors and exposed nationally to cable executives. By stepping up to each new opportunity and giving it her all, she was able to help build Oceanic into the 11th largest cable company in the country.

Networking and hard work were critical to Burr's success. On the networking front, Honolulu was a magnet for executive

RANDY SCHUSTER

More defining moments that shpaed the character of Top Business Leaders.

visits. High level managers and directors loved to do site visits to combine business trips with pleasure vacations. Burr was able to impress them with her knowledge of the business and effective management of her operational responsibilities. This led to national awards for innovation and the development of new processes for the young cable TV industry.

She notes, **"Networking is important, but so is really understanding your role and really going after the challenges that are presented to you."** Burr feels that working outside your area of expertise and being open to doing so is critical for success. Burr says if she had one piece of advice for young people it is this, **"When someone says, 'Would you like to go do something,' take those opportunities because you never know where they might lead in the future."**

Burr also gives a great deal of credit to hard work. **"Do your job 150% so that no one knows it better than you. That's when people start opening up doors for you and offering you opportunities."**

Doors were indeed opening for Burr. Oceanic entered into a partnership with Time Warner Cable, and Burr became

RANDY SCHUSTER

More defining moments that shpaed the character of Top Business Leaders.

the telephony point person. When Time Warner Cable later acquired Oceanic, she was working full-time, caring for three boys under 12, and finishing up her MBA in pursuit of greater opportunities. She went to night classes and spent weekends doing homework. Burr remembers **"It was hard, but you set goals for yourself and find a way to meet them. If it's important, then you find ways to achieve them."**

Seeing her track record of success and noting her recent educational attainments, Time Warner Cable offered Burr a position as division president in San Diego. She would be the first woman to serve as a division president in Time Warner Cable history, if she would move her family to San Diego and take the job.

Burr was ready for new challenges. Her role in the San Diego market harkened back to her past telephony experiences, as she was tasked with building a new competitive telephone exchange company along with managing Time Warner's cable television business. She was able to do it, creating a model for cable telephony services around the country and developing Time Warner Cable's overall product suite into the top cash producing market in the country.

She stayed in San Diego for 10 years, doing much more

RANDY SCHUSTER

More defining moments that shpaed the character of Top Business Leaders.

than just work. Burr was heavily involved in community and industry groups, developing relationships and giving time to causes she felt were important.

"If you're not involved in your community, you are missing out on a great deal of opportunities," states Burr, and she has made it a point to be involved in every place that she has lived. This includes Rochester, where she moved at the prompting of Time Warner Cable executives, who invited her to help build up their telephony and cable television business in the Rochester market.

Arriving from the west coast in the mid-1990s, Burr found Rochester to be a vibrant market and an inviting community. Though she had to look the town up on a map when she first heard of the opportunity, she knew there was a pioneering environment in the city that she wanted to become a part of. She stayed in Rochester full-time for three years, and then took on a national telephony position with Time Warner Cable that had her commuting back and forth between Rochester and Stamford, CT.

Burr loved her job, but was worn out by the travel. Her Rochester roots had deepened through her marriage to A. Vincent Buzard of Harris Beach, and she contemplated

RANDY SCHUSTER

More defining moments that shpaed the character of Top Business Leaders.

retirement. She transitioned out of Time Warner Cable as a full-time employee and launched a consulting business.

She was not on her own for long. A colleague from California, now Chairman at Frontier Communications, Maggie Wilderotter, invited her to join the company where she has been since 2005. Currently she is regional president overseeing Frontier's voice, video, and data communications in NY and PA. This cemented her place in Rochester and allows her to give more completely to the many organizations in the Rochester area that she supports.

Looking back on her journey through life, Burr notes **"I've been very fortunate in being offered new opportunities and new roles, but in taking those roles and opportunities, I have also been very fortunate to grow professionally and personally."** Going forward, Burr sees no slowdown in her future. **"I love to be very busy, love working under a lot of stress, love working with customers, and as long as I can contribute value I'm going to work."**

RANDY SCHUSTER

More defining moments that shpaed the character of Top Business Leaders.

MONEY LESSONS

Along with her time, Burr has been able to give support financially. Her family had moved frequently in her youth, and they lived a modest life. Her breakthrough realization with money came when she understood that she could be responsible for herself, and that working hard to achieve success in business was the most important thing, and this in turn benefited her entire family.

"You can certainly never take it for granted," Burr says of money, and she's always counseled her own children to be thrifty and not spend more than they have. In this way, they can use their money as a tool to support themselves and their families, enjoy a comfortable lifestyle, and still be able to give back to the community.

RANDY SCHUSTER

More defining moments that shpaed the character of Top Business Leaders.

Suzanne Clarridge

President and CEO – My Brands

"Reduce your plan to writing...the moment you complete this, you will have definitely given concrete form to the intangible desire."

Napoleon Hill

SUZANNE CLARRIDGE HAD ENTREPRENEURSHIP IN HER BLOOD, BUT LIFE WASN'T AS SIMPLE AS JUST OPENING HER OWN BUSINESS. INSTEAD, SHE PURSUED DIFFERENT PATHS THAT ULTIMATELY HELPED HER WHEN HER BIG IDEA WAS BORN. BRINGING IT TO LIFE HAS BEEN AN INTENSE JOURNEY, BUT ONE SHE HOPES WON'T BE ENDING ANYTIME SOON.

A Rochester native, Suzanne learned about business around the dinner table. Her father founded Rochester Instrument Systems, starting from scratch to create a large and successful firm. Witnessing his frustrations, stresses, and his ultimate successes gave her an appreciation of the tough realities of doing things on her own. **"My father really instilled in**

RANDY SCHUSTER

More defining moments that shpaed the character of Top Business Leaders.

me that you have to work for what you want. You're not entitled to a living - you're not entitled to anything. You have to work and appreciate the value of your effort."

Suzanne got the message and found a job for herself at a young age. She wasn't allowed to be a papergirl, so at 15 she started waitressing at Uncle John's Pancake House, a job she likes to think of as her first foray into marketing and understanding how to develop and serve consumers.

Suzanne learned very quickly that waitresses make money off tips, which are driven by three things: the size of the check, the quality of the food, and the quality of the service. Two of those things waitresses have control over. She learned to prompt customers to order beverages and desserts, and she became an expert at converting cranky, demanding patrons into loyal clients, skills she would apply later to her own business.

Still, it would be several years before Suzanne would have her own business venture. She had a few twists to navigate first. Chief among them was college, and choices that seemed to lead her away from her entrepreneurial roots. She started as a vocal music major, and transitioned to political science when her major was eliminated. However, neither major

RANDY SCHUSTER

More defining moments that shpaed the character of Top Business Leaders.

seemed to be getting her where she wanted to go.

After college she was back working at restaurants and realizing that she was going to have to get serious and get a degree that made sense. She enrolled at RIT to get an MBA. She paid for the degree herself, and was surprised and grateful after her graduation when her father gifted her some of his company stock.

Encouraged by her professor Jim Mason, Suzanne started teaching at SUNY Brockport. She loved it, but quickly realized she couldn't to do it forever because of the low pay. She debated about going back for a doctorate, but instead chose to put the things she had learned from her MBA program into practice. Suzanne ultimately chose to let her love for consumer packaged goods shine, and convinced Harry Voss, to let her work for him at Diamond Packaging. It was an entrepreneurial environment, and it opened a new set of doors for Suzanne, eventually leading to a job at Mobil Chemical Company in the Hefty Bag division. Her first day, Jim Butler, her boss, asked her where she saw herself in 10 years. Suzanne confidently replied that she would own her own company.

While some bosses might take that badly, Butler thought

RANDY SCHUSTER

More defining moments that shpaed the character of Top Business Leaders.

27

it was great, and he became a life-long mentor and guide. The world of consumer-packaged goods is notoriously demanding, stressful, and full of exacting needs, but Suzanne loved it. With Butler's guidance, she learned about business culture and sought out her niche in the industry.

Suzanne was looking for her big idea. "To be an entrepreneur, you've got to have that big idea, that unique point of difference that separates you from the rest," she says. After a few years with Hefty, the company had a problem that was her inspiration for her big idea: Customers were having trouble getting Baggies in some areas, and they were calling and writing letters to Hefty to try and get exactly what they wanted. Suzanne saw it as an opportunity - anyone who could fill that gap between loyal customers and product distribution networks was going to be meeting a serious need.

Even though this was her aha moment for her business, Suzanne didn't make an immediate move. She had a good job, and a good career . . . and she knew the challenges of an entrepreneurial life. Jane Glazer founder of QCI Direct, one of Hefty's customers who had an existing direct-to-consumer sales model, helped solve Hefty's dilemma. Suzanne watched carefully. She knew if consumers felt so strongly about something as simple as plastic bags,

RANDY SCHUSTER

More defining moments that shpaed the character of Top Business Leaders.

they would be even more passionate about pet products, cookies, or cake mixes.

On July 1, 2000, Suzanne sat down to do her business plan. She'd left Hefty for Fisher-Price, and quickly left that to return to Rochester. She was ready to start My Brands, an Internet based, direct to consumer business.

Her timing couldn't have been worse. By the time she completed all the paperwork to apply for investment monies for her idea, the technology bubble had burst. She was actually laughed out of the room at investor meetings. No one wanted a piece of an Internet based business now, and Suzanne had to decide to go back to work for someone else.

She had already spent quite a bit of her own money, but she didn't want to quit. She decided she could bootstrap the business up off the ground. She quickly rewrote her business plan and started approaching her connections. Jim Butler at Hefty was now in a position to make the firm her first customer, and then B&G Foods signed a contract at their first meeting.

My Brands was still an undefined operation, but now it had clients. Suzanne approached Terri Mentzer, a former

RANDY SCHUSTER

More defining moments that shpaed the character of Top Business Leaders.

29

colleague from hefty, and Laurie Twombly, whom she knew from her network, to see if they would join her. They agreed, Suzanne found an office, and their first order of Baggies shipped out on June 1, 2001.

It was a very basic operation, but they were building things up and continually adding new manufacturers. Though she wasn't taking a paycheck, Suzanne was supported by her husband, Tom Letourneau, and the business got extra support from Judy Seil, a Director with the Monroe County Economic Development Division.

In mid-January of 2002, My Brands got a huge break. Nestle was interested in coming on board . . . but that wasn't the only big news. On January 31, 2002 Suzanne learned that she had a very aggressive form of breast cancer. The doctor recommended that Suzanne quit her business and focus on fighting her illness.

"Giving up is not in my DNA," says Suzanne, and her fight with cancer certainly illustrated her drive. With the support of her husband and a cot in her office, Suzanne kept on growing My Brands through two surgeries, chemotherapy, and the loss of all her hair. Her immune system didn't always allow her to fly, so Terri drove her to sales meetings

RANDY SCHUSTER

More defining moments that shpaed the character of Top Business Leaders.

as far away as Chicago. Instead of dying, in 2002 both the company and Suzanne grew stronger.

By 2003, the company was making money. They put up their website, and expanded their lines even further. Now Suzanne focuses on keeping the business running strong, and her cancer is considered cured. She loves her work and plans to continue to grow her firm over the next decade.

MONEY LESSON

Suzanne's entrepreneurial background gives her a unique perspective on money, especially as it relates to running your own company. **"With respect to entrepreneurship, if you think that somebody is going to write you the big check and you are going to be able to sit back in your office . . .that is rare and highly unlikely in this day and age."** Hard work, bootstrapping it, and controlling costs are critical to avoid debt. **"The one hard and fast rule is to always run in the black."**

"In your professional and personal lives, there is always something else you could spend money on," but Suzanne notes that living within your means is important, as is saving for your future. Money is a tool for investing and creating opportunities. She would not have been able to create My

RANDY SCHUSTER

More defining moments that shpaed the character of Top Business Leaders.

Brands without her savings, and states that no matter how strong the temptation, you have to find a way to control your spending.

RANDY SCHUSTER

More defining moments that shpaed the character of Top Business Leaders.

32

John Cortese

President and CEO of Cortese Automotive

"Practice does not make perfect. Only perfect practice makes perfect."

Vince Lombardi

MOST TEN YEAR OLDS HAVE NO IDEA WHAT'S GOING ON IN THE FAMILY BUSINESS, BUT ONE OF JOHN CORTESE'S EARLY TURNING POINTS OPENED HIS EYES. THE EXPERIENCE SHAPED HIS OUTLOOK ON LIFE AND HIS APPROACH TO BEING A CAR DEALER'S SON. THOUGH HE HAS GONE ON TO BE SUCCESSFUL, FROM HIS TURNING POINTS IN LIFE HE APPRECIATES THE FRAGILE NATURE OF SUCCESS AND THE HARD WORK NEEDED TO KEEP A BUSINESS AFLOAT.

John's story actually starts in a snow bank long before he was born. His father, Pat Cortese, drove a salt truck for the City of Rochester in the brutal winter of 1966. Losing control of the vehicle on a downhill slope on a bitterly cold night, he trudged home through waist deep snow to his pregnant

RANDY SCHUSTER

More defining moments that shpaed the character of Top Business Leaders.

33

wife. Distraught at not having been able to reach him for hours and horrified at the close call, she put her foot down, "You have to find a different job!"

By the time John was born, his father was well into his new career selling cars and later became a manager. Recruited by Dale Scutt to work at his dealership, Pat Cortese took a leap of faith and obtained generous financing to buy his own store when that dealership was up for sale. John was in kindergarten at the time.

Leveraged to the hilt, John's father worked six days a week to make the business work. John rarely saw him outside of the dealership, but remembered that the business was doing well enough for the family to own a set of snowmobiles.

In 1980, Chrysler went through their first bankruptcy and went to Congress for a billion dollar loan, unprecedented at that time. John was 10 years old. With his mother, he added a new line to their nightly prayers, "and please let Congress fund Chrysler." Without the funds from the government, the family finances would be devastated. "Mom," John remembers asking, "if Chrysler doesn't get the money, do we have to sell my snowmobile?" She replied, "If Chrysler doesn't get the money, we will have to sell a lot more than the snowmobiles!"

RANDY SCHUSTER

More defining moments that shpaed the character of Top Business Leaders.

For the first time, John realized that simply being successful one minute didn't guarantee success the next. Even though Congress ultimately came through for Chrysler, John never forgot that things could change and nothing should be taken for granted.

After the bankruptcy scare, John decided he wanted to spend more time with his father, so he would ask his mother to drop him off at the dealership whenever she could. To keep him busy, his father would have him clean cars. John asked for other things to do, gradually getting to know each area of the company and getting a taste of the car business. In those days, he hadn't consciously chosen to go into the business - he just knew he liked it.

This turned out to be a good thing because he was about to start spending a lot more of his free time there. When he was 16, his parents gave him a car with a job attached. He worked 5:00 p.m. – 9:00 p.m. Monday thru Thursday and 9:00 a.m. – 6:00 p.m. on Saturdays at the dealership to earn his gas money.

Many of his friends didn't understand. "Aren't you guys loaded?" they would ask. "With your last name, you should

RANDY SCHUSTER

More defining moments that shpaed the character of Top Business Leaders.

35

be taking it easy!"

John laughed it off or brushed it aside as best he could. Outsiders didn't understand, but in his family there was no easy street, no free ride, and definitely no free lunch. If he wanted anything, he had to work for it, putting in hours at minimum wage.

After school, on vacations, and in the summer, his place was at the dealership. Though it may have seemed shocking to others, in John's family everyone worked. His father was adamant that his children would have opportunities, but that they were never going to get a handout. As a result, John rotated between areas of the company, doing a summer in the parts department, spending time as a lot man, working in the service department, and logging hours in accounting.

In his senior year in high school, John had to write a paper describing where he wanted to be in one year and in twenty years. John was confident that he wanted to be selling cars and to take over his father's business. He had a vision of what he would look like, what his life would look like, and what the business would be like when it was his, and he wasn't afraid to dedicate himself to that vision.

When he graduated from high school, John immediately

RANDY SCHUSTER

More defining moments that shpaed the character of Top Business Leaders.

began selling cars just as he had planned. He loved the work and didn't want to leave it or his high school sweetheart and future wife, Stacy, so he enrolled in RIT rather than going away to school. His parents supported his decision to pursue higher education, but were dismayed when he decided not to finish at RIT.

John had focused on his goal, selling cars, and was doing too well to dedicate himself to his classes. He completed his business education with selected classes at Bryant & Stratton, but opted not to take a degree there, either. He knew what he wanted, and it wasn't a paper hanging on the wall. It was a successful business - his father's, to be exact. **"I just really loved selling cars and working with people."**

Watching other people run "his" business was painful for him. John had never worked anywhere else and he wanted to be the next person in charge. Still, he knew he had to work for it rather than expect it to be handed to him. When his father offered him a management position in the used car department at age 20, he wasn't sure he was ready, but took the chance to learn more of the management side of the business.

John worked in used cars for four years before approaching

RANDY SCHUSTER

More defining moments that shpaed the character of Top Business Leaders.

his father to take over the Dodge dealership. It was the biggest dealership they had at the time. John laid out the case for why he would be the best man for the job, and at the age of 25 he convinced his father. The company went on to have some of its best years.

Looking back, John confesses that he was surprised his father gave him so much responsibility at such a young age. Many other second generation dealerships around them were failing as the younger set lacked the proper work ethic and dedication. **"He put me in the ocean without a life raft, and he figured if I could swim to shore I'd make it, and if not, he'd have to come rescue me."**

Fortunately, John didn't need rescuing. Instead, in his early 30s John started the process of buying the business from his father. In keeping with their family tradition, there were no freebies in the transition. Still, John is appreciative of the opportunity that was available to him, and remains committed to keeping the family business alive.

"The way I have always looked at it, my dad handed me a race car that won lots of races. Now I am racing against different people, so my job is to just keep tuning the race car, and not only not crash it, but make it better." He

RANDY SCHUSTER

More defining moments that shpaed the character of Top Business Leaders.

considers his mark on the company to be the way it has expanded and improved under his management, and wants to be sure he maintains a quality business to pass on to the next generation.

RANDY SCHUSTER

More defining moments that shpaed the character of Top Business Leaders.

MONEY LESSON

For John, money is a secondary effect of working at something you love and are passionate about. **"I didn't get into the car business for the money, I got into it because I liked it, and the money just happened to come from doing it well,"** he notes. He's found that for many people who get into something just for the money, the fun of having that money wears off very quickly, leaving them stuck doing something they don't like each day.

"Money does not make you happy - many people equate money with happiness and the two really have nothing to do with each other," John says, noting that you need to find your happiness elsewhere in life by focusing on the truly important things, like your family, your friends, and doing the right thing. *"Money can be a tool that makes life easier, but you have to respect it. You can't let it control your life. Having money is like the icing on the cake, but it never replaces the cake."*

RANDY SCHUSTER

More defining moments that shpaed the character of Top Business Leaders.

Eileen Coyle

CEO & President of Monroe Ambulance

"Be the best of whatever you are."

Douglas Malloch

EILEEN COYLE HAD ALWAYS DREAMED OF BEING A LEADER. MARRYING JUST AFTER HIGH SCHOOL AND HAVING SIX CHILDREN PUT HER ON A DIFFERENT LIFE PATH. AT 39 SHE FOUND THAT THE LEADERSHIP OPPORTUNITY SHE'D DREAMED OF AS A CHILD WAS STILL SOMETHING SHE COULD GRASP, THOUGH IT CAME TO HER UNDER LESS THAN IDEAL CIRCUMSTANCES. BY TAKING A NEW MARKETING APPROACH SHE WAS ABLE TO BUILD A THRIVING, AND RESPECTED AMBULANCE BUSINESS.

As a small child, Eileen shared a middle-class home with her two siblings. Her father had emigrated from Germany in his late teens and married a Rochester native, working as a steel company foreman while Eileen's mother stayed at home. From a young age, Eileen relished leadership roles.

RANDY SCHUSTER

More defining moments that shpaed the character of Top Business Leaders.

She always wanted to be the one that was at the front of the pack or in charge of others. Taking a job with Kodak right out of high school was her only career experience until her late 30s. She married at 19 and immediately started her family of six children.

Eileen's husband owned an ambulance company as well as a medical supply firm. When her youngest child started kindergarten in the mid-1970s, Eileen went to work at his ambulance company part-time doing dispatching and routing. She deeply enjoyed the work, not realizing that it would eventually become her life's pursuit.

Ambulance services were different in the past, with multiple companies providing EMS response in a fiercely competitive and challenging economic environment. In 1975, large debts and uncollectible accounts forced Eileen's husband out of business, but they still had an ambulance certificate that was not being used. Eileen was approached by their attorney, who asked if she would consider opening an ambulance company in her name. Without a job and with no income, Eileen agreed to take her chances.

She was 39, with no connections and little working knowledge of the industry. Monroe Ambulance had few employees and faced stiff competition in a period some now

RANDY SCHUSTER

More defining moments that shpaed the character of Top Business Leaders.

call "the ambulance wars." Still, Eileen could see potential in the ambulance business and wanted to make it work. Her husband concentrated on his other business pursuits, letting her go her own way to work things out. She laughs now, remembering that he thought he might step back in if things picked up. That never happened.

Instead, Eileen took the company in a whole new direction. At the time, the norm in the ambulance business was to chase emergency patients, with a premium on "scoop and run" trips to hospitals rather than patient service. There were few standard business operating procedures, and many firms operated in a decidedly informal manner.

Eileen envisioned a firm that was professional, organized, and offered Cadillac service to hospitals and non-emergency patients along with emergency field work. She wanted her business to be respected in the community and offer professional service to patients. Rather than fighting for emergency calls from the field, she worked to develop relationships with local hospitals and nursing homes. It was more of a niche business, but she felt it had value.

At the same time, Eileen made an effort to raise her profile through networking. **"I had to be known and the company**

RANDY SCHUSTER

More defining moments that shpaed the character of Top Business Leaders.

had to be known." She went to every community event that she could, even though she vividly remembers not knowing a soul at the first event she attended. Undaunted, she kept going to everything she could. **"Eventually people started to think I was important, because they kept seeing me everywhere, and I started to get invited to join different committees and really get involved in the community."**

Her organizational ties and connections proved to be valuable. Eileen gained friends in other industries and business insight from other entrepreneurs like herself. **"I really learned an awful lot from everybody,"** she remembers. Even though the ambulance business was traditionally a man's business, and she knew no other woman who owned an ambulance company, help was readily available. She remembers men from inside the industry as well as bankers, lawyers and accountants who took the time to show her the ropes, and she was also thankful for the support of various women's organizations during the intense early years of her company.

It was certainly a busy time. As the 1970s came to a close, Eileen's business moved from just making it to thriving. Monroe Ambulance won a six year contract with the City of Rochester for ambulance services. The company was gaining recognition in the community, and Eileen remembers the

RANDY SCHUSTER

More defining moments that shpaed the character of Top Business Leaders.

1980s as a time that the firm really came into its own. The 911 system was put into place while they had the city contract, keeping patients streaming through their doors and promoting growth at the firm.

When the contract with the city expired, Eileen saw the potential end of their existing business model. She wasn't going to quietly go under - that didn't match her competitive style. Instead, she and her team brainstormed about new services that they could offer to set themselves apart and remain a viable business.

They ultimately launched a program known as Medic 42. Named for the number of the ambulance that anchored the program, it provided on-call ambulance paramedic services for hospitals and other ambulance firms responding to emergency calls. In those days, many ambulances didn't have a full EMS staff, particularly on the west side of Monroe County. They needed Eileen's "fly car" of rapid responders to join them for serious cases and true emergency runs. As a result, Monroe Ambulance was able to provide a valuable service to the public, keep costs down for other firms who could leverage highly trained staff on an as-needed basis, and boost their own reputation in the community.

RANDY SCHUSTER

More defining moments that shpaed the character of Top Business Leaders.

The success of the concept was validated in 1990, when the firm won the New York State EMS Agency of the Year Award. **"That was one of the biggest things that we ever did,"** Eileen recalls. The on-call program is still in place today around the county. Innovative moves like Medic 42 and a commitment to service kept the company growing.

Over the years, five of Eileen's six children have worked for the business in one capacity or another. In 1995, three were named vice presidents and Eileen shifted the management responsibilities to a collaborative board approach. One daughter works in the finance department, one son is in charge of the ambulance and the advanced life-support, and another son is in charge of non-emergency operations, the wheel chair business, and the garage. It's a structure that has worked well for them, and allowed the firm to grow to nearly 300 employees.

Looking back, the road from an unknown firm to a thriving business was paved with a commitment to quality service and a willingness to get involved in the community. **"This company would not have been one that you would have bet on to make it, but it did, due to the hard work and loyalty of family and employees. We survived and made a profit, and as all survivors we can say, it's a wonderful**

RANDY SCHUSTER

More defining moments that shpaed the character of Top Business Leaders.

place to be now," Eileen states.

Eileen has not stopped her community work in the Greater Rochester area over the years, giving back and mentoring others just as she herself was supported and mentored. Though at one point it seemed her youthful dreams had been traded for another path, she has definitively seized her second chance and become the leader she aspired to be as a child.

MONEY LESSON

When it comes to finances, Eileen feels that the best advice that she can give to kids is that **"Nothing is free. You have to earn it - it isn't just given to you."** She's found throughout her life that hard work pays off in terms of both finances and goal achievement. **"If you want something, you've got to work for it, and that's how you get wherever you want to be. If you want more, do more."**

She feels that anyone can be successful if they have the fire in their belly necessary to get things done. **"Act like a woman, think like a man,"** is something she's said over the years as advice to women in business, and she's come to appreciate the advantages that financial prosperity can bring. She uses money as a tool to buy back her personal

RANDY SCHUSTER

More defining moments that shpaed the character of Top Business Leaders.

time in the sense that she no longer has to do everything herself at the business, and can now do more of what she wants to do with her life.

RANDY SCHUSTER

More defining moments that shpaed the character of Top Business Leaders.

48

Ken D'Arcy

President and CEO of Crosman Corporation

"If it's meant to be it's up to me."

Terri Gullick

IN HIS YOUTH, KEN D'ARCY LED A NOMADIC LIFE TRAVELING WITH THE FAMILY FOR HIS FATHER'S WORK. CARAVANNING THROUGH HIS FORMATIVE YEARS, KEN LEARNED A NUMBER OF KEY LESSONS AND HONED HIS SKILLS AS A MASTER ADAPTOR AND CHANGE AGENT. WHEN HIS SPORTS CAREER CAME TO AN END, HE FOUND THAT HIS DRIVE AND ABILITY TO TURN THINGS AROUND MADE HIM UNIQUELY SUITED FOR A NON-TRADITIONAL WORK PATH THAT WOULD TRANSFORM HIM INTO AN INDEPENDENTLY DRIVEN SUCCESS.

Ken's childhood was shaped by his father's job in the oil industry, working in seismology and exploration as a geologist and a geophysicist. As a family, they caravanned around with a group of twenty or thirty other families in

RANDY SCHUSTER

More defining moments that shpaed the character of Top Business Leaders.

tiny New Moon trailers, moving from oil site to oil site in the backcountry of Canada and the Upper Midwest. Though others would have called it a hardship, Ken remembers it fondly, reflecting on the community of the groups and the manner in which constant travel can be an effective educator about life in general. He learned to adapt, to change, and to make an effort to fit in to a new community, all lessons that would pay off for him later in life.

Unlike his father, Ken didn't have a strong academic bent. He refers to himself as a "hideous" academic, noting that he preferred to play sports rather than study. The family had settled in Canada when their traveling phase ended, and Ken spent his school years building an impressive athletic stat sheet. He had great respect for his father's intellect, but didn't feel drawn to school. In fact, he didn't know what he wanted to do with his life.

He did know that he loved sports, and he opted to play professional football straight out of school. However, 11 operations later, he knew he needed to find a new career. Ken's other love was ski racing, and he was a ranked racer and top instructor. Linking his love of sports together with the need for an income, he decided that what he would really love to do was open a sporting goods store. To gain

RANDY SCHUSTER

More defining moments that shpaed the character of Top Business Leaders.

experience, he went to work in ski shop.

Ken was still in his early 20s, but a hard reality was sinking in. He didn't like dealing with retail customers. He couldn't handle all of their never-ending demands, and he didn't really like dealing with the public. Yet it was the job that he had. Riding back from his brother's bachelor party with his father, they got to talking. Conversationally loosened by celebratory toasts, Ken's father - by now a successful President at an oil company - blurted out, "I hate my job." Ken was shocked. From the outside, his father's situation looked great. "Why don't you do something else?" Ken asked. "I can't," replied his father, confessing an unrealized dream of being a bookstore owner. For Ken, the moment clicked with something deep inside, and he vowed to never take a job that he hated.

His father was dead a few short years later at 57, his dream of a bookstore still ethereal at his passing. Re-focused, Ken addressed his career with a new mindset. He switched into the wholesale side of the sporting goods business, determined to become the best person in the industry. His personal nature left no room for being anything but good at what he did. He was willing to put the time and effort into his work to become outstanding in his field, building relationships with his clients and making things work. He

RANDY SCHUSTER

More defining moments that shpaed the character of Top Business Leaders.

became a well-known salesman, pulling in big numbers from small territories.

At this point in his life, Ken was successful at work, but he chafed at the idea of always having a boss. Still single, in a disagreement with his sales manager, Ken told his manager he ought to be fired since they couldn't come to an agreement. Management didn't disappoint, and showed Ken the door.

However, six months later, the owner of the company approached him. The company was now in trouble, and having axed the sales manager, they wanted Ken back in a vice president's position. Ken returned, gaining his first experiences as a turnaround leader. Things had progressed too far to save that firm, but a follow-up recruitment by AMF, another major sports wholesaler, and his own joy in the work convinced Ken that his future lay in corporate turnarounds.

Ken devoted himself to work, moving between companies and helping organizations revive their operations. In his spare time, he also studied martial arts, which crossed over into his business philosophy. Helping with a black belt test, he was surprised to see the master award a black belt to a student who lacked natural talent in the art. However, the

RANDY SCHUSTER

More defining moments that shpaed the character of Top Business Leaders.

master made a speech to the class, pointing out that while this student had no great gift for martial arts, he had the passion for the discipline that allowed him to put in the effort needed to become skilled, and this perseverance was what qualified him for the black belt. This reminded Ken of what he had learned in his own life, **"You can't be good at everything, but perseverance will allow you to be okay at whatever you set your mind to."**

As part of his work, Ken traveled, though in better style than his father's caravan crew. For one assignment, he and his family moved to Lyon, France. They were the only English speaking people there, which was a hardship for his 10 and 12 year old children. Yet moving back to Denver, his son confessed that he missed France. "I thought you hated it there!" responded Ken's wife. "No, it was kind of cool," said his son, illustrating another lesson Ken has found to be true over the years. **What seems difficult at the time or maybe not so neat can often turn out to be a pretty big deal in your life.**

In 2001, Ken was asked to leave Denver and come to Rochester by Crosman Corporation. He was 50, and his children were in their teenage years. Crosman was an old firm that traced its history back to 1923, but the thinking at

RANDY SCHUSTER

More defining moments that shpaed the character of Top Business Leaders.

the firm had become stale and sales were flat. The company was privately owned but hadn't made a profit in years, and the owner wanted Ken to turn things around and prepare it for sale.

In agreeing to a six month turnaround gig, Ken didn't anticipate that he would be spending nearly 10 years at the firm. He has managed it through three different sales to private equity groups, and tripled the size of the firm.

Ken credits his success to his abilities to sell the vision of what the firm could be and his ability to develop strong relationships with the vendors and clients of the firm. He empowered internal managers to bring the potential of the company to life, and cultivated long-standing relationships with firm partners. Ken has always felt that relationships are truly critical, and that they grow through personal involvement with others and a concern for other's needs and well-being.

Going forward, Ken knows that he's not ready to lead an inactive life. As long as he is having fun, he plans to keep working, either at Crosman or another firm where there is something interesting to do.

RANDY SCHUSTER

More defining moments that shpaed the character of Top Business Leaders.

MONEY LESSON

He also hopes to pass on what he has learned about money to others. **"You can't have everything today."** He feels that young people, especially those in the US compared to the rest of the world that he has seen in his travels, tend to see what older people have acquired over the course of a lifetime and think they should have it now. **"It's okay to start where you are and move yourself up. It makes no sense to get yourself into unreasonable debt - it's the all-time killer of companies and it makes life miserable for individuals. You will appreciate things more when you have saved for them and paid cash for them."**

RANDY SCHUSTER

More defining moments that shpaed the character of Top Business Leaders.

John DiMarco, Sr.

Chairman and CEO of The DiMarco Group

"You've got to ask! Asking is, in my opinion, the world's most powerful-and neglected-secret to success and happiness."

Percy Ross

HUMBLE BEGINNINGS, DOUBTS FROM THOSE AROUND HIM AND TIMES WHEN HE FOUND HIMSELF WITHOUT A JOB OR A PLAN COULD HAVE ALL LED JOHN DIMARCO TO A DIFFERENT PATH IN LIFE. INSTEAD, HE USED THE LESSONS OF HIS CHILDHOOD, STRONG FAMILY RELATIONSHIPS AND PERSISTENCE TO MAKE HIMSELF A SUCCESS AND BUILD A BUSINESS HE COULD PASS ON WITH PRIDE TO THE NEXT GENERATION.

Echoes of the past surrounded John DiMarco, Sr. as he was growing up in the 1940s and 1950s. His family was struggling to build themselves back up after suffering devastating business losses in the early years of the Great Depression.

RANDY SCHUSTER

More defining moments that shpaed the character of Top Business Leaders.

Instead of living in the house that his maternal grandfather built in 1919, they lived very modestly two doors away, telling stories of the past.

An immigrant from Abruzzi, Italy, his grandfather founded a construction and real estate firm in 1910, created a small fortune for the family and then saw it utterly destroyed. The home and the memory of what once was normal - success, money, nice things - stayed with them in everything they did, influencing John's early years.

A major turning point in John's life came when his mother died when he was 8 years old. "I don't think there is a bigger disaster than losing a mother at an early stage," he says, noting that no one replaces the things a mother does. She had been sick for a little over a year, and as a result of her death and the family's deteriorating financial circumstances, John learned early that, "You have to do for yourself, you have to protect yourself, and anything can happen."

John's father was determined to keep the family intact and get them moving - forward. **"I learned a person can survive,"** John says, **"You can live around these things - I am proof that you can."** He and his brothers continued to live with their father, a strong man and a business owner.

RANDY SCHUSTER

More defining moments that shpaed the character of Top Business Leaders.

Looking back, John knows he challenged his father on some of his business ideas, a situation made possible by their long history as business partners. From a very young age, John knew he wanted to work in the family business. However, his father was extremely cautious as a result of the family's history of losses, and this conservativeness manifested itself in the way he operated his mason contracting business.

One example was their red dump truck. It was purchased new and John remembers walking with his father over to the dealership to buy it when he was just eight. John's father was insistent that it be a small dump truck rather than full-sized, so he could use it for business in residential areas and have it double as his office. The custom-built red Ford truck was a major purchase in 1950 . . . and it stayed a part of the business until it died 10 years later.

The truck colored John's youth as well since it was the moveable symbol of the family business. Not wanting his children to be out unattended on the streets, his father would load them into the dump truck to take them around with him. He figured they would stay out of trouble and learn about business from the exposure.

RANDY SCHUSTER

More defining moments that shpaed the character of Top Business Leaders.

John did learn from his father and also from working construction at a young age. Despite his clear love for the work and his conviction that he was a natural born real estate construction businessman, his father did not encourage him to follow in his footsteps. Instead, he was told he would have an easier and much more comfortable life as a professional man.

John firmly believed that the reverse was true, and the three years at St. John Fisher College didn't dissuade him. He already had a taste for business and earning money and knew that he was more suited to be a businessman than a professional.

His first real estate transaction happened in 1962, when he was just 19. He was too young to personally sign the paperwork for the deal. His father had declined an opportunity to acquire four run-down commercial properties, but John and his older brother Richard thought they had the time to rehab the properties and make them work. So John partnered with his brother, persuaded his father to sign the paperwork, and launched himself into business.

It was successful, not monumentally so, but still a strong start. John was pleased, but his father was not. He wanted

RANDY SCHUSTER

More defining moments that shpaed the character of Top Business Leaders.

59

his son to do well and doubted that things would work out in the long run. The family's history was again a haunting force, as his father was waiting for him to have the same over-extensions and problems that had ultimately disgraced his grandfather.

John wasn't going to let that happen. He continued to do smaller deals throughout his early 20s. In 1967 he found himself ready to propose to his future wife, Debbie, armed with a beautiful diamond, a brand new Buick, $500, but no job.

"I woke up and said to myself, where are you going?" *John remembers.* **"I had no job, no income . . . I had been attempting to do several different construction and development projects but wasn't getting anywhere."** *He realized he needed to really focus on growing the business if he was going to make things work. In the next three months, he and his brother went out and booked more than $1 million in new work.*

His father preferred to operate in a way that he could control in order to avoid risking the losses of the past. He had resisted previous attempts to get him to expand, fearful of another devastating loss. Yet for some reason, this time it was different and he did not object to the accelerated

RANDY SCHUSTER

More defining moments that shpaed the character of Top Business Leaders.

growth.

In short order, John set a wedding date, left dump trucks for a formal office, and dramatically expanded the business. Today the DiMarco Group consists of four separate businesses, has 450 employees and a $200 million book of business.

Still, even as John grew the business, he was prudent about its expansion. They kept significant cash reserves on hand to help weather storms and never took on more than they could handle. While some might have said it was overly cautious, John credits his father's fearful guidance with steering him and Richard onto a path that has prevented the DiMarco Group from taking any major losses for 45 years. "Now people tell me I am lucky," laughs John. "It didn't happen overnight."

More than the financial success, John is pleased about the family success. **"I've had people say to me all my life, how can you work with your family? Don't you want to be independent?"** Yet he can't imagine anyone better to work with and counsels young people not to overlook the pleasure and value of working with those you trust and love. He and his brother Richard have been life-long partners,

RANDY SCHUSTER

More defining moments that shpaed the character of Top Business Leaders.

61

and John feels that one of their greatest achievements is that they have been able to pass the baton to their children during their lifetimes. **"I didn't want my children to wake up one day and find out that they have X amount of dollars, or remember me as a money hungry father who was just amassing dollars."** Instead, the children were involved in the business from a young age. They were welcome to come to meetings and were all given individual responsibilities. John considers his children's continuation of the family business tradition to be their greatest success story.

RANDY SCHUSTER

More defining moments that shpaed the character of Top Business Leaders.

MONEY LESSON

Growing up as he did, John learned many lessons about money. **"It boils down to one word: Realism. Don't play pretend. Life is wonderful if you live within the parameters that you should,"** he says. If you spend more than you have and behave irrationally with money, there are consequences. Just like drinking or partying, the consequences of poor choices can be expensive and painful.

Another important lesson for kids is to not cross their financial lines. If there is money to be set aside for a rainy day, do it and leave it alone. **"You don't have to be a frugal nut and never enjoy life,"** John says, but in his upbringing and throughout his business career he has learned that having cash reserves can protect you from misfortune and help you find new opportunities.

He also reminds kids that you don't need to own the world, as you can't keep it. **"One day we all pass away and you leave everything you have right here, so don't ruin life relationships over a few dollars because it's just not worth it."** John counsels that relationships are much more valuable than money!

RANDY SCHUSTER

More defining moments that shpaed the character of Top Business Leaders.

Tom Dustman

President of Vekton Corporation

"A man's life is what his thoughts make of it."

Marcus Aurelius

ALWAYS PUSHED TO GO TO COLLEGE, TOM DUSTMAN SEEMED TO BE ON A STRONG UPWARD PATH. EARLY BUSINESS TURNING POINTS PUSHED HIM OUT ON HIS OWN, BUT IT WAS A TURNING POINT IN A HOSPITAL THAT TRULY FOCUSED HIS PRIORITIES. NOW, HE CELEBRATES BOTH LIFE AND BUSINESS SUCCESS.

Growing up in Buffalo, NY, Tom Dustman had the opportunity to learn all the words to "Tiny Bubbles". The song played nightly on the jukebox of the bar across the parking lot from his parent's rented apartment. Though his parents worked hard, home ownership was not something they pursued, and so each night he would fall asleep listening to bar music.

RANDY SCHUSTER

More defining moments that shpaed the character of Top Business Leaders.

Yet despite what some would call hardship, Tom remembers his old neighborhood fondly and credits his youth with inspiring him to set goals to have more and be more. The youngest of three with two older sisters, Tom had a loving environment at home and a constant encouragement to pursue college from his mother. His father provided a strong example of a dedicated work ethic, going to work each day as a milk deliveryman, seldom taking a vacation.

Between his mother's insistence that he go to college and a talent for basketball, higher education seemed like a natural next step for Tom after graduation. He was the first of his family to go to college, starting at a junior college before being recruited to RIT.

Playing college ball was a dream come true, and moving from junior college to RIT was a good fit for Tom. In addition to equipping him with a business degree, he was also introduced to three quality mentors and role models. Bill Carey, the coach who recruited him, Roger Dykes, RIT's Sports Information Director, and Lou Spiotti, the RIT Athletic Director, all shaped a part of his future.

Tom credits Bill Carey with giving him confidence by showing an interest in him as a player and as a person. Roger Dykes invited Tom to share a home with several other athletes

RANDY SCHUSTER

More defining moments that shpaed the character of Top Business Leaders.

who would become his good friends, and gave him guidance when he needed it as he made his way through school. Lou Spiotti went on to become the best man at Tom's wedding, and opened many doors for him.

After graduating, Tom continued his business education by pursuing an MBA. However, he interrupted his studies when an opportunity came to play professional basketball in Europe. Though it seemed like a dream come true for a lover of the game, Tom quickly found that the culture shock was harsh and the environment wasn't one that he wanted to stay in long-term.

Returning to Rochester, Tom knew he needed a job - fast! He answered an ad in the paper to do sales for a construction company, earning himself a position in door to door sales. He honestly admits that in the beginning, he was a failure.

The first three months, Tom took home just $634 in commissions. One day, he came home and had a talk with himself about the situation. Though he briefly considered quitting, he decided that he wouldn't give up. He could see others were successful - others with fewer educational and personal resources than him. He talked with himself, remembering his father's example of simply going to work each day, and decided that there was no reason he

RANDY SCHUSTER

More defining moments that shpaed the character of Top Business Leaders.

couldn't do the job.

Making a stronger commitment to the work, Tom underwent a transformation from a sales loser to a sales leader. He started teaching sales tactics and sales management within the firm, and to this day some of his sales protégés are still making a good living in the industry.

He credits some of his advancement and success to people at his company who were willing to take him under their wing. Tom firmly believes the old adage, **"When a student is ready, a teacher arrives."** People could see that he was hungry and ready to learn, and so they reached out to share their knowledge with him. Tom soaked up everything he was taught so that he could do it on his own.

His personal resiliency quickly became important. Leaving his first firm and first success, he joined another business as a minority owner, but was pushed out. He had a young son, Tom, a wedding in the works, and no income to rely on. He took a job with a commercial construction firm doing marketing, but was fired. Rather than going back to depending on others, he decided to strike out on his own. Partnering with a man he had trained in sales at his previous firm, Roy Gordon, Tom launched his own company, Vekton

RANDY SCHUSTER

More defining moments that shpaed the character of Top Business Leaders.

Corporation. He was confident in his own abilities, and trusted Roy, who was hard-working, loyal, and had previous construction experience. There was so much to do, Tom reflects, that there was never time for doubt or to be scared. The duo worked well from the start, and since 1986 has been among the Top 500 members of their industry, with recognition from qualified remodelers across the country.

In 1991, Dustman was diagnosed with non-Hodgkin's lymphoma. He was 35. His cancer was in the third stage when it was discovered. Tom got his diagnosis and began to prepare himself for the end, thinking, "I have already had a very full life. I've played basketball, traveled, been married, had a beautiful child. I could prepare myself to die."

He felt fortunate to have experienced so many good things, but his mind drifted to the others in his life. His wife, Kate, was a special force in his life, grounding him and making him whole - but she would be okay without him. His partner, Roy, just needed to be told a few things about the business and he would be fine running it. His son, Tom, was 10 years old and - he suddenly realized that without a father, his son wouldn't be equipped with everything he would need to go to college and be successful in life. How could he even consider just giving up and dying?

RANDY SCHUSTER

More defining moments that shpaed the character of Top Business Leaders.

Determined to fight, Tom made it through six months of chemotherapy without missing a single day of work. As a result, his cancer is gone, and he has happily attended his son's high school and college graduations. He has also had the opportunity to have a daughter join his family.

After the cancer, Tom and Kate tried unsuccessfully to have another child. After a series of ectopic pregnancies and failed in vitro sessions, they considered adoption. However, Kate's sister offered to serve as a surrogate carrier for the couple. Tom initially opposed the idea, thinking it would be too complicated. Yet as time went by, he warmed to the idea. As doctors had frozen some sperm prior to the chemo in case he became sterile as a result of the treatment, they were able to artificially inseminate Kate's sister, Molly. Tom's daughter, Emma, was born when he was 39.

As his family was growing, so was his business. Over the years, the firm continued to grow and has served more than 12,000 customers. Tom looks forward to working at his business for as long as he is healthy, adding. "I've been very fortunate in life."

RANDY SCHUSTER

More defining moments that shpaed the character of Top Business Leaders.

His own fortunate outcome financially has let his story of success extend to his broader family. Early in his career, before he launched his own business and even before he bought his own home, Tom used his savings to invest in a duplex so that he could move his parents out of their rented apartment. There were to be no more nightly strains of "Tiny Bubbles" for them - instead, Tom's early success enabled him to fulfill his youthful goals of using money to have more and be more in life as a homeowner and someone who was able to provide stability, control, and security for those around him.

RANDY SCHUSTER

More defining moments that shpaed the character of Top Business Leaders.

Lou Fuchs

UniLink, Inc.

"If we are ever to enjoy life, now is the time, not tomorrow or next year. Today should always be our most wonderful day."

Thomas Dreier

LOU FUCHS HAS ENJOYED A LIFE BUILT THROUGH HARD WORK AND SACRIFICE. GROWING UP IN A FAMILY WITH AN IMPRESSIVE WORK ETHIC, HE FACED A MAJOR TURNING POINT WHEN HE WAS IN COLLEGE. LATER WHEN HE LAUNCHED HIS OWN BUSINESS, HE FOUND THAT THE LESSONS FROM BOTH HIS YOUTH AND HIS "WAKE UP CALL" IN COLLEGE WOULD GUIDE HIM TO SUCCESS.

It's a good thing that Lou Fuchs comes from a family that gets along and supports each other, as the first 10 years of his life were spent in a house with more people than rooms. The three bedroom structure was home to eight people - Lou's parents and their six children.

RANDY SCHUSTER

More defining moments that shpaed the character of Top Business Leaders.

Lou's father worked full-time for Bell Aerospace in Buffalo. In addition to working overtime and on the weekends, his Dad sold life insurance to earn additional income. It was a worthwhile effort that paid off in the form of financial success and the ability to move the family to a larger house.

Over time, his father grew his business and eventually formed his own life insurance agency. Yet even though Lou's father went on to achieve significant material success, Lou recalls that his father was never materialistic. His father was always focused on character, honor, and commitment. He was never one to actually talk much about his success - he led by example for Lou.

Hard work was simply expected. Even as a small child, summers meant a "Things To-Do" list for Lou. His father always wanted to make sure that Lou was constantly doing something - painting, yard work, or chores. Tasks had to be done within a certain timeframe and then they could be crossed off the list. From this Lou learned adherence to standards, the value of a job well done, and the importance of making good use of his time.

Yet even with his working background, Lou's first semester at St. John Fisher College proved to be a very challenging

RANDY SCHUSTER

More defining moments that shpaed the character of Top Business Leaders.

time for him. School was a distracting place, and Lou spent more time having fun than studying. At the end of the semester, he posted a dismal 1.7 GPA.

Going home at Christmas was an opportunity for his father to talk with him, but it wasn't a talk that would ultimately change the course of his life. Instead, when his father dropped him off at college for the spring semester, he handed him a note which Lou still has today, safely preserved in his desk at home.

The note described how Lou's grandfather had come over from Germany by himself when he was 13 years old. He was the oldest of 10 children. He was alone and he didn't speak a lick of English. Despite these challenges, his grandfather became a medical doctor. There was nobody to provide him with financial help, but through hard work and dedication he had become successful in his own right. The note closed with a reference as to how the family names on both his mother's side and his father's side were names of integrity and character, and that if nothing else, Lou's father hoped that his son would have integrity and be hard-working.

The note served as a wake-up call for Lou. **"It made me focus on the fact that I wasn't really all that talented. To be**

RANDY SCHUSTER

More defining moments that shpaed the character of Top Business Leaders.

successful I needed to work and be consistent in everything that I did." His spring semester was a dramatic change as he turned his grades around and posted a 3.9 GPA.

After graduation in 1978, Lou went into the life insurance business for two years with Met Life. It was a great experience for him. **"You have nothing, and the people that you are calling have nothing because they are in your age group. But you have to make the calls, go in after hours, set up appointments and work on the weekends."**

During this time, a good friend introduced Lou to the Burroughs Corporation where he worked in information technology for seven years. He had a set of co-workers, Sully, Bill and Tom G., whom he admired and enjoyed being around. From them he learned a great deal about building and growing relationships with customers. He was taught to really care about the customer as a person and to demonstrate integrity in his work.

As Lou turned 30, he decided to start his own company offering multi-manufacturer technology solutions to customers. He operated the business from his one-bedroom apartment, buying used equipment and refurbishing or reconditioning it. He vividly remembers being up late at

RANDY SCHUSTER

More defining moments that shpaed the character of Top Business Leaders.

night scrubbing keyboards and other components with a toothbrush to get them looking good for his customers.

Building the business, Lou enjoyed the support of his wife, Lisa. Though she had a full-time position with Citigroup, she put in hours at night and on the weekends helping with the books and invoicing. Lou remembers one time when they crowded 85 computers into the apartment, putting them in the bathroom, bedroom, kitchen, and anywhere there was an available space.

Even though it was difficult, Lou feels that those were some of the best years of his life, because he really got involved in every aspect of the business. He was also continuing his business principles education with Lisa's father, who had become a best friend and mentor. They would meet for breakfast twice a week, talking about different facets of business, including how to talk to prospects and manage customers. **"Make sure that you are very attentive and take care of your customers, and good things will happen."**

After two years, Lou and Lisa were able to move the business out of the apartment and into their current location, where they have been for over 20 years. A large part of their success comes from customer relationships.

RANDY SCHUSTER

More defining moments that shpaed the character of Top Business Leaders.

"You treat each customer and each piece of business as equally important." Lou considers there to be no greater endorsement than to earn the trust of his customers, and to have them trust him enough to come back over and over again. **"It's an awesome feeling to be trusted by your customers."**

Along with the customer care focus, Lou has found that many of the lessons of his youth have proven invaluable to him as a business owner. He considers the importance of his father's example in many aspects of the business. One illustration of this is in the relationship that he has with his employees.

His father's staff always thought very highly of him, in no small part because of the way that he worked. His work ethic also took him to the Million Dollar Roundtable (the premier association of financial professionals) multiple times, but his real pride was in seeing a member of his staff also make it to the table.

Lou has transferred that mindset into his own business. At his staff meetings, he always makes it clear, **"I would rather sell nothing and have you guys sell everything."** Lou also credits the dedication of his staff to customers and the

RANDY SCHUSTER

More defining moments that shpaed the character of Top Business Leaders.

business for the company's success.

Though he had the opportunity in his life to take a wrong turn when he entered college, Lou now feels that he enjoys an incredibly blessed existence. He hopes that his children and others will internalize the lessons of his story by adhering to the values of hard work, persistence and a commitment to doing the right thing.

RANDY SCHUSTER

More defining moments that shpaed the character of Top Business Leaders.

When it comes to money, rather than a single moment of insight, Lou has learned his lessons over the course of his life. **"You've got to earn it on your own,"** he says. **"You've got to work hard, and you've got to work smart."** He encourages his own children and others to focus on something that they enjoy. He views money as a tool to help develop and grow his business. Lou has found that a commitment to doing the right thing ensures that things will work out, and notes that, **"If you provide great customer service and get a real charge out of it, then the money just follows."**

RANDY SCHUSTER

More defining moments that shpaed the character of Top Business Leaders.

John Gabriele

President Marina Auto Group

"Actions speak louder than words."

Michel de Montaigne

WORKING IN HIS FAMILY'S RESTAURANT BUSINESS THROUGHOUT HIS TEENS, JOHN GABRIELE SWORE HE WAS GOING TO GET A JOB WHERE HE DIDN'T HAVE TO WORK WEEKENDS. HIS PATH TO A "REAL" JOB TOOK A SHARP DETOUR IN 1986. AGAINST HIS FATHER'S ADVICE, JOHN PURSUED AN OPPORTUNITY THAT TOOK HIM ON A NEW ADVENTURE THAT ULTIMATELY LED TO SUCCESS.

John's parents immigrated to the Rochester area in 1955. Ethnically Italian, they had met and married in Brazil. One of his father's cousins enticed the couple to come to the land of opportunity, where both of them started their own businesses.

John was born in 1964. His entrepreneurial parents

RANDY SCHUSTER

More defining moments that shpaed the character of Top Business Leaders.

impressed two important values on him - hard work and education. He went to quality Catholic schools, with college fixed firmly on the horizon. First, however, he had to survive a youth in the restaurant business.

John was 12 years old when he started as a busboy. Just as his father had worked his way up from the bottom of the restaurant business, so too was John expected to start on the ground floor. Nights, weekends, and holidays found John waiting on other families at their restaurant rather than doing sports or socializing. Instead, he learned basic business management skills, how to deal with the public, and that the one thing he wasn't going to do with his life was restaurant work.

John's goal was a formal college education, so he could work for a big company and actually have a day off. He started by enrolling at Monroe Community College, which moved him toward his goal without moving him away from his high school sweetheart and future wife, Mary Ellen, or his regular shifts at the restaurant.

An almost perfect GPA enabled him to move from MCC to St. John Fisher for his degree. John rushed through to finish so he could start the life that he wanted. In December of 1985, he had completed all of the credits for a May graduation

RANDY SCHUSTER

More defining moments that shpaed the character of Top Business Leaders.

with a BS in Management with a finance marketing concentration. He planned to spend the spring applying for his "real" job and working a little bit at the restaurant

However, he was loathe to put in any more restaurant hours. Through his sister, he met Tony Gabriele (no relation) who had a newly opened car dealership in Avon that needed staffing. It was February of 1986, and when the other employees bet that John, with his college education, wasn't going to stick around long, Tony encouraged them to give John a chance.

After training, John sold a car his first day. He still remembers the brand new 1987 Plymouth Horizon America that was his first sale . . . but not his last. He was the top salesman that month, and inside of three months he had earned $10,000 selling cars. Tony took him out to dinner, told him he was a natural, and invited him to head up the dealership's new finance division.

Unfortunately, he had also accepted a commercial lending job with Chase, to start that June. However, running the numbers he could see that his bank salary wouldn't measure up to his car commissions. When his father found out he was thinking of going into the car business over the

RANDY SCHUSTER

More defining moments that shpaed the character of Top Business Leaders.

bank job, he said "What the hell did I spend all that money for sending you to college if you're gonna sell cars?"

Fortunately, Mary Ellen's father was a bit more supportive. He pointed out that John was young, and if the car business ultimately didn't pan out, he could always start over. John agreed, and told Tony he'd do it, as long as he got a company car and at least one day off. Tony agreed, although John laughs now that through personal choice he never did get his day off.

The financial stability of the job allowed John and Mary Ellen to marry in August of 1987 and own their own home from the start. They were saving to buy a lot and build their own house when the opportunity arose for Tony, John, and Tony's sister, Sonya, their other partner, to buy out Weller Motors.

They opened negotiations with Bruce Weller in December of 1988. John was 24 at the time, and Tony only a few years older. Bruce was in his 60s, and he gave the "boys" a non-negotiable price. Over the course of 1989 they hammered out the payment details, with Bruce agreeing to hold paper to smooth the financing. On September 18, 1989, John walked in as an owner, feeling overwhelmed.

RANDY SCHUSTER

More defining moments that shpaed the character of Top Business Leaders.

There was a lot to be done to modernize the business, but John still feels looking back as though Bruce Weller had given a 25 year old the opportunity of a lifetime -to be a business owner. It was a third generation firm when it sold, and the new owners rolled up their sleeves to move the business from 100 – 150 cars a year to 500 cars a year sold.

As the decade ticked by, the business continued to grow. The early 1990s overall were winning years, and John and his partners built their business and their confidence by leaps and bounds. They were expanding rapidly, and in 1995 seized an opportunity to buy Bill Gordon's Chevrolet dealership.

The deal was inked and the team was moving ahead fast. All that was needed was final approval from GM. Never thinking it wouldn't come, the team invested heavily in Gordon's business. Five months down the line, they learned that top GM officials were no longer interested in having a dealership at that location, no matter who was running it. As John puts it, "We took a pretty good hair cut on that one."

He was 31, and it was tough to handle. **"There is no amount of education they give you in college to prepare you for**

RANDY SCHUSTER

More defining moments that shpaed the character of Top Business Leaders.

stuff like that, none. You just have to live and learn from stuff like that, but that doesn't make it any less of a tough pill to swallow."

The team pulled back a bit in the market, and John was grateful for the support of his wife as he figured out what was next for the business. The late 1990s were tough, and the dealership also needed to move out of its primary location in Irondequoit due to a city construction project. Their land was being acquired through eminent domain and the city was set to make a deal with them for a new parcel.

The deal for the new parcel fell through. John's dealership was going to be homeless if it weren't for a community connection that came through unexpectedly. In 1999 he had been asked to sit on the board for the Rochester Auto Dealers Association, where he met the owner of Timothy Dodge. Approaching John, he offered to sell his dealership. Mulling it over, John went for the deal and had the city move his business to Webster in May of 2001.

It was a shining moment for John. After the gloomy late 1990s, the sour GM deal, and the absent Irondequoit parcels, the move let him renew his commitment to the business. He never wanted to work anywhere else.

RANDY SCHUSTER

More defining moments that shpaed the character of Top Business Leaders.

The new location was significantly smaller, and the business quickly developed a need for space. They opened a larger building in 2004 to accommodate their growth. They were in an acquisition phase, targeting a Chrysler Jeep franchise while acquiring a Mitsubishi franchise. Even during the recent belt-tightening years, the business has continued to thrive. They survived the Chrysler bankruptcy, and ultimately acquired their long-desired Jeep franchise.

Going forward, John doesn't see any slowing down. "We're in a growth mode again," he says, noting, "I have some high aspirations for the next 10 years."

RANDY SCHUSTER

More defining moments that shpaed the character of Top Business Leaders.

John also has high aspirations for the next generation - **if they can be responsible with their finances. "One of the big things you learn in my business is the importance of credit and paying your bills on time,"** he says, noting that responsible use of credit can dictate every aspect of future deals and large purchases from cars to homes. Those who are smart about managing their money can get better deals, better finance terms, and lower interest rates.

John often tells his own children that actions speak a lot louder than words, and that achieving financial success is not just about good money management but also the willingness to put in the hard work and make the sacrifices to really achieve what you want out of life. **"Success isn't going to happen by accident,"** he says, and encourages effort and dedication to ensure that the next generation can also meet their goals.

RANDY SCHUSTER

More defining moments that shpaed the character of Top Business Leaders.

John Gay

COO of R. Brooks Associates, Inc.

"There are no gains without pains."

Benjamin Franklin

IF YOU ASKED HIS HIGH SCHOOL TEACHERS, JOHN GAY WASN'T GOING ANYWHERE IN LIFE. YET HE CO-FOUNDED A UNIQUE AND SUCCESSFUL BUSINESS. HE GIVES A LARGE PART OF THE CREDIT TO THE TURNING POINTS IN HIS LIFE WHICH PROVIDED HIM WITH DISCIPLINE, RESPONSIBILITY, AND THE ABILITY TO STEP IN WHERE OTHERS WOULD HAVE BACKED AWAY.

John grew up in Rochester, the oldest of eight children. His grandfather owned Gay's Gym, and his father was a World War II veteran who worked as an appliance repairman with Rochester Gas & Electric (RG&E). John speaks of his family life with fondness.

His mother was always very supportive of him, and they

RANDY SCHUSTER

More defining moments that shpaed the character of Top Business Leaders.

maintain a close relationship. John credits his mother with being a positive influence in his life, noting that she always believed in him. This was true even when John got kicked out of high school.

He was 17, and had failed three courses at Bishop Kearney High School. Girls, sports, and his social life were all more important to him than grades. At the end of his junior year, he was told not to return for his senior year.

Transferring to Eastridge High School, John already had enough credits to graduate. He attended homeroom and negotiated his way out of other classes, spending his days working at a catering company. He was in love for the first time, planned to enlist in the Marines, and just didn't see the value or importance of high school at that time.

Now if you ask him about high school, John has a clear message: **"If you do very well in high school, you get your choice of colleges, you might get a scholarship, and you can choose some different career paths. If you don't do well in high school, you just make your road in life that much harder. If you realize these things while you're still in high school, you are setting yourself up for a much easier time than the kid sitting next to you."**

RANDY SCHUSTER

More defining moments that shpaed the character of Top Business Leaders.

This lesson took some life experiences before John was able to appreciate it. When John graduated from Eastridge, he was simply happy to be done. Wanting to learn some trade skills, he did a year of an apprentice tool and die program before starting with the Marines in 1967.

The three years John spent in the Marines were a major turning point for him. In the Marines, John learned personal discipline, gained a broadened perspective, and received a technical education. "I had to understand and work with others to be successful. Just because I saw something one way didn't mean that it was the right way." My father had always taught me, "Son, understand that you're no better than anyone else and they're no better than you. We're all equals here. Judge people on their merits."

The Marines drove all those lessons home, and by the time John left the service in 1970, he was a dramatically different person than before.

When John left the Marines, he had an avionics education, a sense of personal discipline, a desire to stay in Rochester, and an interest in continuing with his tool and die apprenticeship. Unfortunately, in 1971 the economy tanked. Gillette Machine and Tool laid off more than 100 people,

RANDY SCHUSTER

More defining moments that shpaed the character of Top Business Leaders.

89

including John. He was 23, with a wife and young child to support, motivating him to join RG&E.

RG&E was John's home for nearly 20 years, and he considers it a great company to have worked for as they provided him with multiple opportunities. One very important element for John was education, as RG&E paid for night school at RIT. He earned his associate's degree and got within three courses of a bachelor's degree, proving to himself that he could do well academically.

Another turning point came in 1972 when RG&E asked for volunteers to work at the Ginna nuclear generating station. Ginna station had opened in 1969, and in 1972 many people were terrified of nuclear power. Yet John saw only opportunities.

Being accepted as a volunteer for Ginna marked a significant change. John leap-frogged from a simple gas repairman to someone at the front end of an emerging technology. He further secured a niche for himself by volunteering for another position others shied away from - sludge lancing.

Sludge lancing, a type of tube pressurization and cleaning, was not a glamorous job. Yet Ginna had more than 6,000

RANDY SCHUSTER

More defining moments that shpaed the character of Top Business Leaders.

tubes, providing John with plenty of opportunity to build his knowledge base and establish himself as an expert. He became the go-to guy for steam generator secondary side tube issues, interacting with the highest levels of management and nuclear management teams around the country.

A critical moment came on January 25, 1982. A steam tube sprung a leak, causing an evacuation of the Ginna station that John remembers vividly. As the repair and clean up efforts began, John's unglamorous but essential expertise was in high demand.

There was no technology in the world at that time to examine or fix the issue. As the steam generator secondary side tube man, John was responsible for building the probe system to inspect the area of damage and make the necessary repairs.

From there, additional doors opened. John was introduced to Ray Brooks, an entrepreneur, and the two realized they had the potential to be business partners.

In 1986 they began working together along with three other partners. John kept his day job but worked nights, weekends, and vacation days on the business. Bruce Weir's

RANDY SCHUSTER

More defining moments that shpaed the character of Top Business Leaders.

garage served as the company's headquarters, and for four years John devoted every spare minute to it.

After their first successful outside project, John remembers sitting in his hotel room thinking that his life had definitely changed. He was now an inventor and an achiever.

On July 1, 1990, John celebrated his birthday along with his last day with RG&E. He went to work full-time with R. Brooks, - only to see 1991 arrive with no contracts and $1.5 million in debt. John spent the next four years driving around the country with his partners, selling to every utility they could, and by 1995 they were completely debt free. **"Now we hate debt, because it means someone else is in control."**

The company has certainly recovered. From no contracts, they now have partnerships with Westinghouse, Northrup Grumman, and the Department of Defense. A multi-national, multi-million dollar operation, there are now approximately 100 full-time employees with 100 part-time workers or contractors, and the company is continually expanding and innovating to make themselves and their services better.

Looking back on it all, John recalls how it wasn't until he was

RANDY SCHUSTER

More defining moments that shpaed the character of Top Business Leaders.

in his 30s that he really knew what he wanted to do with his life. He admonishes others, **"Be patient with yourself. Don't worry if you haven't arrived in your mind yet. Keep plugging and working hard at whatever you do, do the best at whatever you do. Learn in the arena that you're working in."**

From his high school experiences and his struggles to make the business a working proposition, he notes **"If you fail, it doesn't mean that it's done. It just means move on and believe you can choose another path."**

The former high school reject is now an enviable success. The lessons John learned have shaped everything he has accomplished but further chapters lie ahead. He may write a book, and he will definitely continue to grow the business. From his turning points, he knows that the future is his to claim.

MONEY LESSON

A key lesson for John is the importance of cash flow and debt avoidance. **"When I first started, if you'd asked me the most important thing in business, I would have told you 30 things before I said money. The reality is that cash flow is the most important part of the business because**

RANDY SCHUSTER

More defining moments that shpaed the character of Top Business Leaders.

if you can't pay your bills, you're out of business." He also thinks that taking on debt in your business is a choice to be carefully made, since being in debt involves giving up control.

John remembers the long hours that his father worked. He vividly remembers his father telling him as a young boy to run his own business if he could, because working for someone else meant that somebody else had to make money off your efforts. The conversation had a big impact on John, helping to motivate him to find his independence.

RANDY SCHUSTER

More defining moments that shpaed the character of Top Business Leaders.

94

Ken Greene

President of Flour City Bagels, Bruegger's Bagel
Bakery's largest Franchisee

---

*"There is a principle ...which cannot fail to
keep a man in everlasting ignorance - that
principle is contempt prior to investigation."*

Herbert Spencer

LOOKING BACK ON HIS LIFE, KEN GREENE FACED A NUMBER
OF TURNING POINTS. HE HAS HAD TO OVERCOME A
CHALLENGING CHILDHOOD AND TAKE LEAPS OF FAITH IN HIS
BUSINESS VENTURES. HIS TURNING POINTS HAVE ALLOWED
HIM TO GROW HIS BUSINESS THROUGH HARD WORK AND
DEDICATION STARTING WHEN HE WAS 26 YEARS OLD.

Starting off with a comfortable life in Massachusetts, Ken
Greene faced his first major turning point when he was
just seven years old. His father and grandfather had been
successful businessmen, but they both declared bankruptcy
in the same year. His world of comfort was shattered as the

RANDY SCHUSTER

More defining moments that shpaed the character of Top Business Leaders.

money disappeared, his parents divorced and he and his siblings moved back in with his mother's parents. Ken lost his sense of security.

Ken's mother worked on reinventing herself, and Ken credits her with teaching him tenacity and determination. She started over, putting herself through college and going on to become a paralegal. Her actions led Ken and his siblings to ask themselves, **"What are your priorities and how are you going to achieve them?"** Still, it was a process, and his teenage years were hard.

Living on the wrong side of the financial divide, Ken felt his diminished status acutely. He attended school in an upscale community as he had before his parent's divorce, but things were different. He was envious of his friends, and that envy became a driving force in his desire to build a comfortable life.

He got his first job the week before he turned 16, working at a Howard Johnson's as a dishwasher. Inside of a year he was managing the kitchen, and during his last two years of high school also had two side businesses going. He made sand terrariums and installed car stereo systems. These businesses laid the foundation for an entrepreneurial life.

RANDY SCHUSTER

More defining moments that shpaed the character of Top Business Leaders.

After high school, Ken went to Syracuse University, where he took his work ethic with him. In his sophomore year he was a resident advisor and president of his fraternity. He enjoyed success in leadership roles during college which set a precedent for his life.

After Syracuse, he went to work for Delaware North in Buffalo, NY, gaining an interview with the company through a headhunter, Moe Roe, who was a family friend. Delaware North handled food service in sports venues and National Parks. Ken worked as a manager of menus and new product development, and found his first mentor in his boss, Bill Dennis.

He would go to breakfast with Bill three or four times a week. Bill treated Ken like a protégé and helped him learn how an organization gets revenues and manages its costs. This was very educational for Ken.

After a few years, Bill Dennis left the firm. Ken subsequently transferred back to Boston, managing the private suites at the Boston Garden, but the environment wasn't a good fit.

A family friend, Harold Traeger, had just taken over the

RANDY SCHUSTER

More defining moments that shpaed the character of Top Business Leaders.

restaurants at Filene's Department Stores, and Ken left to open two new restaurants for him. He had creative control over the process, which he loved. However, after the first year, the restaurants were sold.

Ken called his headhunter friend Moe, asking about potential job openings. Moe mentioned Bruegger's, a bagel company that was just beginning a major expansion. They were offering ownership stakes in the shops for the operators building out the market. Since Ken was only 26, Moe thought that he would be considered too young to qualify for the opportunity.

"Just get me an interview," Ken said. He got the interview, met with the founders, Nord Brue and Mike Dressell, and obtained a contract for the Albany area.

It was 1986 and 75% of the population had never had a bagel. Bruegger's had not yet become a franchisor. Looking back, Ken says that it was an almost unbelievable opportunity for him. **"There are a lot of people out there who are a lot smarter than me, and there are a lot of people who work a lot harder than me. I have not met anyone who is luckier than me."** At 26 years of age, he lacked significant business capital, but he did have his strong work ethic and previous

RANDY SCHUSTER

More defining moments that shpaed the character of Top Business Leaders.

restaurant experience to bring to the table.

He moved to Albany and took over the three existing stores. Over the next four years, Ken grew the business and built another five or six stores in the area. Realizing the market was now up and running, he started looking for growth opportunities. It was at this point that he moved to Rochester.

Ken did not move alone. He had met his future wife, Kimberlie, while working at Delaware North. At one point shortly after he was married, his wife asked him, "Do you have to work seven days a week?" Ken was surprised, as he loved his work and it didn't feel like work to him.

In Rochester, Ken replicated the Bruegger's operating structure and continued to grow the business. Eventually, Ken had the opportunity to buy the remainder of the Upstate NY region's ownership stake from the founders of the company.

As Ken worked with Bruegger's, Nord Brue became his mentor. Ken learned how to buy real estate and get stores opened, as well as additional operating nuances of the business. As a result, Ken's original three store footprint grew to a total of 33 stores.

RANDY SCHUSTER

More defining moments that shpaed the character of Top Business Leaders.

Ken has always used general objectives for the kinds of things he wanted to accomplish in a year, but does not like formal goals. He does, however, take great pride in certain accomplishments, like the creation of the world's largest bagel by his team. Inspired to make the attempt by his son, it allowed him to execute on a major personal principle of, **"Getting a team focused on an idea that is greater than any individual would even imagine as a goal, and helping that team to accomplish that goal."**

Ken also joined the Young Presidents' Organization (YPO), an international group. A small group meets monthly and has become a trusted forum for Ken. The members dig into challenges and successes in work, life, and family areas together.

Going forward, Ken plans to continue to grow his business while pursuing more balance in his personal life. By his reckoning, in 25 years with Bruegger's he has taken fewer than 25 weeks off, and a friend's challenge to take a single day off and do only things that he wanted to do proved difficult. As a result, in the future Ken plans to keep dedicating himself to business success, but will be defining business success as a process that includes more than pure work.

RANDY SCHUSTER

More defining moments that shpaed the character of Top Business Leaders.

MONEY LESSON

When it comes to money, Ken feels that it's all about balance and responsibility. Growing up, he was exposed to a mother who was afraid to spend money for fear that it would all disappear, and a father who was convinced that money would never run out, which it always did. From these two extremes, Ken had to learn his own lessons about money based on trial-and-error, experience, observation, and adaptation.

"I've learned that there are tradeoffs between living for today and planning for the future," Ken says. He encourages others to put thought into finding their own place of financial balance.

RANDY SCHUSTER

More defining moments that shpaed the character of Top Business Leaders.

Jim Hammer

President and CEO of Hammer Packaging

"There is no such thing as a free lunch."

Milton Friedman

JIM HAMMER BEGAN EMBRACING CHANGE AND TECHNOLOGY FROM HIS EARLIEST DAYS WITH HAMMER PACKAGING. YET THE JOURNEY INTO A FAMILY BUSINESS IS NOT ALWAYS SMOOTH, AND MAKING YOUR OWN MARK REQUIRES A WILLINGNESS TO TAKE RISKS. WHERE OTHERS MAY HAVE GIVEN UP, JIM'S TURNING POINTS INSPIRED HIM TO DO MORE, PUSH THE ENVELOPE, AND TAKE A LEAP INTO THE FUTURE.

Jim, who had a younger brother and two sisters, was the second oldest of four children. He represented the fourth generation of Hammers, most of who were involved in the family business, Hammer Packaging. However, Jim's first job wasn't with the firm. Instead, he got his own paper route when he was 10, and kept the job through high school.

RANDY SCHUSTER

More defining moments that shpaed the character of Top Business Leaders.

Through this, he learned how to manage finances and deal with people.

When Jim was in high school, he started working for Hammer Packaging. The business had been founded in 1912 by his great-grandfather, and Jim put in his time on the second and third shifts while he was in high school and college. Summers, holidays, and breaks would find him at the plant. He got to see first-hand how the business worked, and was exposed to the level of investment in machinery and equipment that formed the foundation of the business.

In those days, Hammer Packaging was just a place for Jim to work. He had no great desire to join the family business upon graduation from college. He was working on a business degree in marketing, but had no fixed goals for his post-college years. He didn't really know what he wanted to do.

When Jim graduated, he considered his options carefully. Looking at the family business - then run by his father and his uncles - Jim could see that his father needed help. His grandfather had retired, and the stress of the business was taking a toll on Jim's father, who was serving as president. Jim decided to join the firm to help his father, and to try to improve some areas of Hammer's operations.

RANDY SCHUSTER

More defining moments that shpaed the character of Top Business Leaders.

The firm was loosely organized in those days, succeeding on its merits rather than strict internal systems or the latest technology. Jim wanted to change that. After a few months with the company, Jim got all of the owners together to talk about transition planning and organization. The company had no buy/sell agreements in place, and though everyone held shares, the value of the shares had never been agreed upon. "What will you do if you want to leave the business?" Jim asked, but the idea never gained traction.

In fact, many of Jim's ideas in the early days didn't get far, and he had to ask himself if this was the environment he truly wanted to be in. Impatient and ambitious, the status quo at the business was frustrating him. Still, he stuck with it, hoping for his chance to make a difference and take control.

His two uncles became sick within a few months of each other, forcing the buy/sell issue to the forefront. He ended up buying out his uncle's shares in the early 1980s and became president of the company in 1983. Though the circumstances hadn't been ideal, the opportunity was now his. Jim managed the company as well as he could, moving sales up but realizing that they were constrained by their existing equipment and technology. Upgrading however, would be a substantial capital expense.

It was 1987, and Jim had a decision to make. He could continue to manage a successful firm that was behind the times technologically or he could take an enormous financial risk to upgrade the firm's equipment and processes. The total amount of money needed for just this one project was more money than had been invested in equipment at the firm in total from 1912 to 1987. Jim's father thought he was nuts, so when Jim decided to move ahead, he had to buy his father out of the business completely.

The investment turned out to be the right choice, even if the numbers attached to it were initially frightening. As a result of a continual commitment to technological innovations, Jim was able to grow Hammer Packaging's workforce to over 400 and increase sales from $8,000,000 in 1989 to over $100,000,000 in 2011.

For Jim, it was about more than just the business continuing on to the next generation. He reinvented the company according to his ideals and abilities. Internally, he had a vision of what the company could be and had the passion to help bring that vision to life.

"If you are just sort of treading water you are going

RANDY SCHUSTER

More defining moments that shpaed the character of Top Business Leaders.

backwards. Change is what it's all about," he says. He's established five shared values for the firm that express his vision and his commitment to the future - integrity, respect, trust, credibility, and continuous improvement. Jim also makes it a point to distribute Who Moved My Cheese?, his favorite book about change, to all Hammer Associates and vendor partners.

Training is another key part of his commitment to change and improvement at the company. **"One thing we need to do, is to drive away the fear of change. You have to be proactive about it."** He focuses on training his people with new skills and technologies because he knows that technology will never stop changing the business landscape and the job requirements at his business.

Jim doesn't keep his passion and energy to himself or confine it to his company. He has also made a commitment to being active in the community through the Young Presidents' Organization (YPO) and later the World Presidents' Organization (WPO). Invited into the YPO by its founder, Ray Hickock, when he was in his early 30s, Jim considers the organization to have been critical to his career. It provided him with a forum of peers to serve as supporters, advisors, and sounding boards, and got him involved in youth and

RANDY SCHUSTER

More defining moments that shpaed the character of Top Business Leaders.

106

community business education programming, something he has always viewed as important.

Within his family, Jim feels that **"setting examples and leading by example does more to instill values than just talking about things,"** though maintaining open lines of communication is still very important. He and his wife, Donna, always encouraged their children to make a difference, and though he never pushed the business on them, he is proud to have two of his children working for the company.

Looking to the future, Jim is excited to have the business continuing into the fifth generation. He is also looking forward to keeping abreast of innovations that will require changes at Hammer Packaging in order to keep them at the forefront of their industry. Whatever else he may do, one can be sure that embracing change and welcoming new technologies will play a starring role as the company continues to "Lead, Not Follow".

RANDY SCHUSTER

More defining moments that shpaed the character of Top Business Leaders.

MONEY LESSONS

Jim's lessons about money revolve around the effective management of financial resources. "There's a responsibility that comes with money," he says. Learning to give back based on what you've earned and accumulated, managing your finances, and respecting the effort that it takes to make money are all critical.

The role of the risk-reward factor has also been a strong element in Jim's financial life. "You have to understand what the financial implications of everything are. There's no such thing as a free lunch." Jim says. He has continually used the "power of money" to borrow and reinvest in his business in order to stay competitive, remain on the leading edge of technology, and aggressively grow the business.

RANDY SCHUSTER

More defining moments that shpaed the character of Top Business Leaders.

Michael Haymes

President of RE/MAX Realty Group Incorporated

"If you think you can, you can."

Dan Clark

MICHAEL HAYMES LIKES TO SAY THAT HE WAS NEVER A GOOD STUDENT, BUT HE'S GRADUATED FROM THE COLLEGE OF LIFE WITH A MASTER'S DEGREE IN SUCCESS. BY TAKING HIS FIRST JOB AT TWELVE AND WORKING CONSISTENTLY SINCE THAT TIME TO BUILD SUCCESSFUL BUSINESS VENTURES, HE HAS BEEN ABLE TO PROVE THAT FOCUS, DEDICATION, AND LOTS OF HARD WORK TRULY DOES PAY OFF.

Growing up in Rochester, Michael Haymes had entrepreneurship in his blood. His great-grandfather operated Rochester Smelting and Refining, and living modestly with his mother, grandmother, and two sisters in a fatherless home, Michael grew up with stories of how the business had been founded and grown. He knew from a young age that he liked to work, liked business, and that

RANDY SCHUSTER

More defining moments that shpaed the character of Top Business Leaders.

school was not really his thing.

One of his very first forays into the business world came when he was 12 years old. Central Trust Bank of Rochester launched a Rent-A-Kid program, where kids were hired and sent out into the community to help people at home doing window washing, yard cleaning, or similar chores. Michael was the first one to sign up when the program started, earning his first bit of local business press and a salary of $1.35 an hour.

He was motivated by the opportunity to make money, and even in his pre-teen years he was always aggressively looking for chances to work and earn. Once he turned 14 and could get a proper job, he went to work at Mr. Steak as a busboy and cook. He worked all through high school, happily putting in long hours at his job.

Michael could work for hours everywhere but the classroom. School didn't interest him like the business world, and while he gave college a go for a year, he quickly returned to Rochester. He was interested in the restaurant business, and worked at the Changing Scene while looking for other opportunities.

RANDY SCHUSTER

More defining moments that shpaed the character of Top Business Leaders.

Keeping his ears open and building his network, Michael met Max Springut, a local real estate broker and restauranteur. Max's family owned the Red Creek Inn, and was in the process of buying Don & Bob's. He asked Michael if he was interested in buying into the restaurant, since they were taking on partners. Only 21 and with little capital of his own, Michael got his mother to co-sign a loan for him to get into the business.

Don & Bob's proved to be a smart move for Michael. Within five years, he had paid off his loan and saw the business grow five-fold. It wasn't luck - Michael worked relentlessly at the restaurant, putting in 10 and 12 hour days on a regular basis, with Tuesday afternoons as his only time off.

All those hours weren't spent alone. Max Springut shared a small 10 x 15 foot office with Michael in the back of Don & Bob's, doing real estate deals. It was a window into another kind of life, and one that was increasingly attractive to Michael.

He had met his wife, Karen, during his restaurant years. When they married in 1984, Michael was coming to the realization that his new life and the restaurant business were not going to be a good fit. As he looked for other opportunities, it seemed that real estate was everywhere in

RANDY SCHUSTER

More defining moments that shpaed the character of Top Business Leaders.

111

his life. Max was doing commercial real estate deals, and his mother, now in Florida, was a successful residential realtor in Boca Raton.

With his best friend from childhood, Jeff Hoffman, Michael joined a small independent real estate company. Jeff had been in real estate since getting out of college, and Michael was willing to work to catch up. They had been working together for a few years when Michael's mother told them about RE/MAX, a growing real estate franchise that was thriving in Florida but not yet in New York State. Jeff and Michael contacted RE/MAX, learning more about them and getting on their list as a first point of contact when the New York licensing was approved. After the approval, they met the regional director in Buffalo to give him a check to buy a RE/MAX franchise.

In hindsight, Michael laughs that when they were writing the check, they didn't know what they were getting themselves into. RE/MAX worked differently than other real estate groups in the Rochester area. It was a commission based system, with agents getting 95% of the proceeds and chipping in each month to cover agency overhead. For confident sales agents with a good production record, it seemed like a winning proposition.

Michael and Jeff opened their office in August of 1987,

RANDY SCHUSTER

More defining moments that shpaed the character of Top Business Leaders.

thinking it would be easy to recruit other agents to work with them and have the business take off. They chose an attractive location and furnished 15 individual offices with beautiful furniture. Looking the part and ready to work, they were expecting success.

It did not come easy, and recruiting agents was hard. The different business model wasn't attractive to everyone, and competition was stiff. Jeff and Michael focused on building their brand, targeting highly visible listings to get their name out. Things were slow initially, and Michael had a lot of sleepless nights over their finances.

Fortunately, his family believed in him and his ability to make it work. Michael's father-in-law gave him unflagging support, and his sister joined the company as an agent, as did Jeff's brother John. They invested in training seminars and focused on expanding their network of relationships in Rochester. Bit by bit, the long hours and the networking began to pay off for them.

Through sheer persistence and hours of relationship building, the office grew. In 1993, Michael and Jeff were named as the international Broker Owners of the year for a single office by RE/MAX International. Since that time, they

RANDY SCHUSTER

More defining moments that shpaed the character of Top Business Leaders.

have been the number one sales office in New York State for 17 years in a row, and now have more than 100 agents in a 12,000 square foot office.

Looking back, Michael knows that things could have gone differently. People were always calling him to get involved with other ventures and different causes. However, as he sees it, **"The fact that I allowed myself to focus on RE/MAX Realty Group really was the catalyst in taking us through all these years because I didn't get involved in anything else for 15 years."** Once he started the business he was committed to seeing it through, even though it meant years of late nights and working 80 to 90 hours a week.

"If you focus on what you are doing and surround yourself with good people it's going to work if it's the right thing," he says, thankful for his business partners and the relationships he's built over the years. With his focus, passion, and drive, there's no end to the possibilities, and Michael looks forward to what the future holds for him and his business.

RANDY SCHUSTER

More defining moments that shpaed the character of Top Business Leaders.

MONEY LESSON

Michael's money lessons began at home. Living with his grandmother, he was very influenced by her take on money. **"Money is round and it rolls,"** she would say, **"It rolls away from you unless you are doing something to bring it your way. You have to respect it, and you must know the value of a dollar."**

Working as he has, Michael has certainly learned the value of a dollar, but he also values the balance. **"You need money to live, but doing what makes you happy is more important than having money and not being happy,"** he says. He considers himself fortunate to have grown up with a healthy respect for money and to have found a career where he can be happy with what he is doing and still be prosperous.

RANDY SCHUSTER

More defining moments that shpaed the character of Top Business Leaders.

Tom Judson, Jr.

Chairman and CEO of The Pike Company

"The secret to success in business is to manage the cost of failure, not the frequency."

Anonymous

TOM JUDSON SEEMED TO HAVE A SMOOTH PATH PREPARED FOR HIM IN LIFE. FROM AN EARLY AGE, HE KNEW HE WANTED TO JOIN THE FAMILY BUSINESS. BECOMING PRESIDENT AT THE FIRM SEEMED TO BE A FULFILLMENT OF THAT GOAL, BUT INSOLVENCY AT 40 HADN'T BEEN PLANNED. WITH RESILIENCE, DETERMINATION, AND A SOLID SUPPORT NETWORK, HE WAS ALLOWED TO TAKE A "GAME OVER" SCENARIO AND TURN THE BUSINESS BACK INTO A SOLID SUCCESS.

Looking back on his youth, Tom Judson feels fortunate to have enjoyed such a positive childhood. He had a loving family that was blessed with financial security, and he had access to a high quality education throughout his youth. In

RANDY SCHUSTER

More defining moments that shpaed the character of Top Business Leaders.

the back of his mind was always the family business, John B. Pike & Son, where Tom planned to spend his days when the time came.

In the meantime, he made the most of his school years. In high school, he developed a bit faster than his peers, enabling him to make varsity teams as a sophomore in football and lacrosse, though he ruefully admits that by his senior year his peers caught up with him. From high school, his academic success got him into Yale, and he later went on to Cornell for post-graduate work.

While at Cornell, he married his long-time friend, Ebets, in June of 1968. He considers their marriage to be one of the defining elements of his life as well as one of the best things he's ever done. Tom maintains that he has never regretted it or wanted to be with anyone else the entire time they've been married.

After graduating from Cornell, Tom was looking to join the family business. Tom's older brother and younger brother had pursued other opportunities out of college, leaving the option and the opportunity open for Tom to join the business. He never had any doubts that it was the path for him.

RANDY SCHUSTER

More defining moments that shpaed the character of Top Business Leaders.

He had started with the business in the form of part-time summer work when he turned 18 in 1963. Having never worked elsewhere and with no wandering eyes for other ventures, Tom dedicated himself whole-heartedly to the growth and development of the firm.

Descendants of the original founder had worked at the business continuously since 1873, and Tom strove to keep up with the legacy of success. At first, fate smiled, and the company enjoyed a strong period of success and growth. In 1975, when Tom was only 30 years old, he was named President and Chief Operating Officer.

The sunny path continued for a few more years, but by 1985 the firm had suffered a series of projects gone wrong and industry-wide economic adversities that left them insolvent.

The future seemed bleak. Tom had two small children at home, Rufus and Bess, as well as an entire network of family members and employees who based their livelihoods on the company. Since becoming President, Tom had convinced his brothers to leave their jobs to join the company in a period of rapid expansion. Overextended with operations in

RANDY SCHUSTER

More defining moments that shpaed the character of Top Business Leaders.

multiple states, the business faced the end of its road.

Tom felt as though he had let everyone down. It was terrible and he felt very guilty. Looking back, he says that he can't imagine having felt worse, and he treasured the constant support of Ebets and his family as he tried to work through the situation. He was 40 years old and starting over from square one.

Fortunately, not everything was against him. The bonding company supported Pike through the completion of all the firm's outstanding projects so that no customers were hurt, something that Tom could feel good about. His surety also supported him in the launch of The Pike Company, which wouldn't have been possible without their backing.

He started fresh with limited resources, taking on one project at a time. The brush with insolvency had taught him to consider more carefully than ever the nature of the project, the nature of the client, and the risk-reward potential. Their first successful project was the Woodcliff Hotel, and the business built up incrementally from there.

His employees were tremendously valuable to him as he rebuilt. **"I don't know how to do anything very well, but I have been very successful at surrounding myself with good**

RANDY SCHUSTER

More defining moments that shpaed the character of Top Business Leaders.

119

people," Tom states. He had faith in his people, and never doubted that they could make a second go of the business.

Relationships were critical in the rebuilding, since the firm is basically a service business. Establishing relationships, ensuring they were positive and oriented for the long term, and filling those relationships with value bolstered the firm. One time projects turned into repeat business, and the touch-and-go beginning grew into a steadily increasing stream of customers.

Overall, Tom feels that although it was a tough road at the time, both he and the business came out strengthened by the experience. **"I think people who have not had bad experiences don't have as much to offer as those who have."**

From around 40 people as a skeleton staff starting over, Tom has built The Pike Company to over 400 employees. He has also played an active role in the community, volunteering with a number of organizations and working with the Rochester Business Alliance in several roles, including as the RBA chairman.

Going forward, Tom is pleased to already have his son, Rufus

RANDY SCHUSTER

More defining moments that shpaed the character of Top Business Leaders.

and his son-in-law, Mauricio Riveros as the next generation working productively in the business and to have the company's legacy continue. **"My life has been one of great success,"** he says, noting that while he has had some tough experiences, in the balance it has been very good, and he looks forward to filling the years ahead with interesting projects and interesting people.

RANDY SCHUSTER

More defining moments that shpaed the character of Top Business Leaders.

MONEY LESSON

When it comes to money, Tom cultivates an attitude of gratitude and thankfulness toward finances in his own life and has a message for the next generation. **"Money is very hard to earn. You need to be aware of how you do, and you need to be providing a real service that's valued. If you can do that, it's pretty cool."**

In many areas of life, money is the essential operational lubricant and the means of keeping score on successes. Tom has found that most of his projects revolve around a three-legged stool of quality, timeliness, and cost. To this support framework, Tom adds a fourth leg which is the experience of doing business. He feels that a large part of what enables his business to continue to grow and thrive is providing his customers with a good work experience and a product that they truly enjoy and value when it's delivered.

RANDY SCHUSTER

More defining moments that shpaed the character of Top Business Leaders.

John Krueger

President of HEP Sales and North Main Lumber

"Attitude, to me, is more important than facts...I am convinced that life is 10% what happens to me and 90% of how I react to it."

Charles R. Swindoll

OPPORTUNITIES LOST AND OPPORTUNITIES SEIZED. THESE TWO THINGS CAN MAKE A DIFFERENCE IN THE STORY OF A LIFE, AND THEY CERTAINLY MADE A DIFFERENCE IN THE LIFE OF JOHN KRUEGER. FROM HIS YOUNGER, AIMLESS DAYS TO HIS CURRENT FOCUSED LIFE, OPPORTUNITIES HAVE BEEN A CONSISTENT PART OF HIS STORY.

John was born in 1961, the youngest of four boys. His mother was a school nurse and his father was an independent electrical contractor, who described himself as a fabulous electrician but a horrible business man. He wouldn't follow up on overdue bills, and he shied away from confrontation. From an early age, this colored John's perspective to make

RANDY SCHUSTER

More defining moments that shpaed the character of Top Business Leaders.

123

him feel strongly that working hard should be rewarded.

This lesson about the value of work was followed by a lesson about the importance of opportunity. John's mother had two brothers who invited his father to join them in a new venture. However, his father declined based on loyalty to John's mother's foster father, who had a competing contracting business. While John's uncles became extremely successful, John's father stayed where he was, and John could see that the missed opportunity was a constant disappointment.

In the late 1970s, John's father was diagnosed with lung cancer. He died in 1979, when John was just 17. It was very hard on the family emotionally. Often unsupervised, John chose to be a B student and run wild. He had no real passion for anything, and though he enrolled in a two year program at Alfred State College, he had no idea what he wanted to do with his life. John simply lived day to day, enjoying himself. He was taking data processing his first semester, and failing four out of his five classes.

John's mother had a chat with him, though he already knew that data processing wasn't working out. He switched into business administration and did better, but he didn't have any plans to be in business at that point. His oldest

RANDY SCHUSTER

More defining moments that shpaed the character of Top Business Leaders.

124

brother had taken over the family business, and John wasn't terribly interested. He just knew he needed a degree and he recognized college as a protected environment where he could stay until he was ready for the real world.

He finished the two year program at Alfred, earning his associates degree and went on to SUNY Brockport, where he enrolled in a Human Resources program. In the meantime, his fiancé, Chris took a job with Canandaigua National Bank and moved in with John's mother while he finished school.

SUNY Brockport proved to be a different experience from Alfred, as John got interested in his classes. He graduated in 1983 with cum laude honors. He was excited to work, since a professor had told him, "When you get out there, don't accept any job that pays less than $45,000 a year." It was a very decent paycheck for the early 1980s, and John began dropping resumes at big name companies he thought would be a good fit for him.

John vividly remembers the complete and utter feeling of rejection when he applied for jobs and received no responses. Throughout May and June of 1983, he job hunted. He was planning to marry Chris in July, and he really wanted a job before they were married.

RANDY SCHUSTER

More defining moments that shpaed the character of Top Business Leaders.

In July, the phone finally rang with a job offer. It wasn't from any of the firms in Rochester where John had applied. Instead, it was John's uncle, George Sullivan, the owner of HEP Sales. His offer was simple, "I would like you to come to work for us as soon as you get back from your honeymoon."

From his first day in August, John remembers two things. The first was a complete and utter feeling of despair when his uncle told him his salary - it was peanuts. The second was how it felt to spend the day with his cum laude education up on the steel roof of a building in 105 degree heat applying tar to screw and nail holes that had popped.

On his way home, John thought, "What happened to my $45,000 a year human resources salary and college education?" Still, he was happy to have a job, and in the back of his mind he was sure a big company would call soon. This was an opportunity to get a temporary paycheck while John figured out what he was going to do with the rest of his life.

After three days of roof work, John's uncle sent him to fill a retail store position in Auburn, NY. It meant a commute, but John did not object. In fact, as John recalls, **"If he asked me**

RANDY SCHUSTER

More defining moments that shpaed the character of Top Business Leaders.

126

to do something, I did it without question. It was not mine to question, the man was extremely successful, he knew what he was doing, and if he told me to work on the roof in 100 degree heat, I assumed there was a reason why he needed me there and that is why I did it."

John loved his experience in the retail environment. Like a sponge, he soaked up information about retail operations and management styles, learning something everyday. After two years, his uncle gave him the opportunity to manage a store. Success there provided more opportunities as John thrived in the retail environment.

In 1987, John's brother approached him about rejoining the family business and made him a generous financial offer loaded with benefits. John felt torn. He didn't feel he would get along working with his brother long-term, but he also didn't feel he would survive a life in retail stores. After talking things over with his wife, he went to talk to his uncle. "Are there further opportunities for me here?" he asked. "Absolutely," his uncle replied. John didn't mention his brother's offer to his uncle until later, after he had turned it down.

Generous financial package aside, John felt that staying with his uncle was the right thing to do. There were more

RANDY SCHUSTER

More defining moments that shpaed the character of Top Business Leaders.

opportunities at HEP if he could be patient. The decision proved to be the right choice, as John was later made operations manager, and got to put his Human Resources training into practice. They built job descriptions, set performance metrics, and tightened up internal operations. In 1989, John became vice president.

Also in 1989, John's son Max was born. Until that point, John had never put much thought into the future. Suddenly, how John lived directly impacted his son's quality of life. It was a huge personal awakening. He focused himself, developed goals and a clear cut purpose, and put his energies into the business.

Over the next few years, John's uncle developed Alzheimer's disease, and John took over as president, handling 100% of the business operations and eventually buying his uncle out. In 1999, the company had the opportunity to dramatically expand, and John took it. Over the next 11 years, HEP doubled their workforce and number of locations, tripled sales, and took the number of products they sold from 6,000 to 37,000.

Reflecting on the total journey, John feels grateful for the passion and drive in his life. **"I am a firm believer that you**

RANDY SCHUSTER

More defining moments that shpaed the character of Top Business Leaders.

need to be passionate about something in your life, if it brings you happiness, solitude, or success - as long as you are not hurting yourself or others, passion in my opinion is the fire that provides the necessary focus." In his time at HEP, John has been able to thrive with his passion for the business, and to be proactive instead of just letting life happen to him. "I believe that I need to always be moving forward - and this is truly important - I must do the next right thing, whatever that may be." At HEP, he feels he is surrounded by extremely talented people that he can trust, that he can rely on to be very good at what they do, and whom he can allow to make decisions to grow the company and seize opportunities.

What matters to him most today is his wife, his two sons Max and Daniel, and his work. He feels that everything he enjoys now results from hard work, staying focused, and realizing his primary purpose in life. "If I can do those things, I truly believe I can do anything."

RANDY SCHUSTER

More defining moments that shpaed the character of Top Business Leaders.

MONEY LESSON

As a result of his personal emphasis on passion, hard work, and purpose, his view of money is that it is to be used as a tool, not a goal to achieve. **"Money is a commodity, a means to an end. It's the opportunity to do the things that you want to do in life,"** he says. In his own family, he teaches his children to be grateful for what they have, and to understand that if they want to be successful in this world, then money is a necessity that must be earned. **"If you want to be successful, figure out what it is that you bring to the table that is going to allow you to be successful in whatever you do to earn a paycheck,"** John says. In this way, he feels that you will be able to grow your business, care for your family, and sleep at night because all of the bills are paid - just a few of the key opportunities money can buy.

RANDY SCHUSTER

More defining moments that shpaed the character of Top Business Leaders.

Joe Lobozzo

Founder - JML Optical Industries Incorporated

"The second you think you've arrived, someone passes you. You have to always be in pursuit."

Joe Torre

JOE LOBOZZO HAD A HUMBLE START, AND A FUTURE IN OPTICS WAS THE LAST THING HE EXPECTED WHEN GROWING UP IN THE SOUTH BRONX. OWNING HIS OWN BUSINESS SEEMED UNTHINKABLE TO HIM AS A CHILD. AN ENTREPRENEURIAL SPIRIT COMBINED WITH AN OPPORTUNITY IN HIS SENIOR YEAR IN HIGH SCHOOL WOULD BOTH GREATLY INFLUENCE HIS FUTURE.

The South Bronx has never been known as a place of wealth and privilege. Growing up there, Joe Lobozzo was exposed early to the challenges of paying the bills and keeping food on the table. He and his sister shared a modest apartment with their father, a $50/week railroad clerk for the New York,

RANDY SCHUSTER

More defining moments that shpaed the character of Top Business Leaders.

New Haven, and Hartford rail systems, and their mother who juggled family responsibilities with part-time jobs. The family struggled financially, which made a big impression on Joe.

At a young age, he went to work. His uncle distributed fuel oil, and Joe helped him out on weekends and in the busy winter months. All through his teens, Joe put in hours whenever he could, watching and learning as his uncle expanded the operations of the company he founded.

The contrast between the way the two families lived was obvious to Joe. Working for someone else like his father, he could eke out a living his whole life, renting an apartment and stretching dollars to make ends meet. If he worked for himself he could live like his uncle, owning a beautiful brick home outside the Bronx and purchasing new cars. The entrepreneurial seed was planted as Joe realized that to be really successful, you have to do it yourself.

As he grew older, his mother found a way to send him to All Hallows, a private Catholic boy's school. Joe has no idea how she managed to have the $30/month tuition, but she was never late. The school had a strong reputation with some 99 percent of the students going on to college.

RANDY SCHUSTER

More defining moments that shpaed the character of Top Business Leaders.

Joe was an above average student, though he didn't always apply himself as diligently as he could have. Science and math came easy to him, but he didn't have a fixed idea of what he wanted to do with his future.

One afternoon in his senior year, his biology teacher and guidance counselor, Mr. Fiordalisi, invited the students to hear a guest speaker on optics. It was his fiancé, Sandra Wender Hoffer, a German-accented beauty. The boys stayed with permission to ask her anything except her phone number . . . and for Joe, it was the start of a serious infatuation . . . with optics!

Sandra Wender Hoffer worked for Fairchild Camera, and she provided an intriguing overview of the opportunities available for jobs in optics. She personally was designing lenses for space study, and with the Vietnam War just beginning, there were opportunities to obtain a draft deferment for those working in the field of defense-related optics. Joe was intrigued by the nuances of the design requirements, and remembers being absolutely sold that day on optics as a career. **"I'd never thought of it once before that day and never thought of a different career path since then."** He marvels at how different his life would have been if he had not had the opportunity to attend Ms. Hoffer's presentation.

RANDY SCHUSTER

More defining moments that shpaed the character of Top Business Leaders.

Optics classes at the next level meant college, and college meant tuition money, which Joe didn't have much of to spare. He was accepted to all the schools he applied to but due to the tuition costs he ultimately chose the City College of New York, which would only cost him $300 per year for his major in physics with an optical emphasis.

When Joe graduated, Boeing was recruiting in New York City for optical jobs in Seattle. They made him an offer, but he found the thought of leaving his extended Italian family so far behind overwhelming. Ultimately he took a job in Chicago, reasoning that it wasn't nearly as far.

Around 1970, Joe came to Rochester in pursuit of a master's degree at the University of Rochester. His company had offered to pay for it, and Joe naively thought that he would be able to maintain his sales engineer's schedule with traveling two weeks a month and still pursue the degree. With travel to both the east and west coasts, the master's degree quickly became problematic. However, scheduling wasn't the only snarl in Joe's life at that time.

By 1972, the many broken promises at his current employer were getting under his skin. They had a great product in a growing industry, but they could never seem to deliver. It

RANDY SCHUSTER

More defining moments that shpaed the character of Top Business Leaders.

134

was tough for Joe to reconcile his personal ethics and skill at selling with the backend issues he knew would hit his customers. Joe felt that management didn't understand the value of providing good customer service. He knew that he could provide a quality product and better service on his own and convinced his wife at the time, Joanne, that now was the time to start his own business.

JML Optical Industries operated out of the garage in Joe's backyard at his home on Genesee Park Boulevard. He had two small children and very little start-up capital, but he was passionate about the potential of the business and willing to pour all of his efforts into making the company work.

It was profitable from the start, and Joe made progress taking customers away from his competition with great service before and after the sale. When Ilex Optical went bankrupt, Joe bought their equipment and building. However, despite net profitability, cash flow was a constant issue. Joe purchased materials from Japan, doing the design work in the US and selling to customers around the country, which created cash flow problems because of the substantial time differential between the due dates of his payables and receivables. These problems kept him up at night.

RANDY SCHUSTER

More defining moments that shpaed the character of Top Business Leaders.

Fortunately, just when he hit his financing limits with his original bank, he met Sherman Farnham Jr., a loan officer at Citibank. The bank was new in town and looking for growing businesses as customers, and Farnham invited Joe to let Citibank meet his needs. Along with the professional relationship, they cultivated a deep personal friendship as Joe continued to aggressively grow the firm.

He worked 18 hours a day at his business, allocating most of his limited free time to his family. He laughs that he must have been a big bore at the time, because even when he was at his kid's games and events he talked about work, and when events were over, it was right back to work. He gives Joanne credit for being incredibly supportive and helpful with their family through those years.

In 1980, Joe joined the Young Presidents' Organization (YPO). He made a number of good friends and connections, and discovered a new passion - running. The group did the New York Marathon each year as a team, and Joe started running 50 miles a week to participate with them. He's now completed 23 marathons with YPO, and credits the experience with helping him find a bit of a balance in his life, since he needed more time to run and sleep!

RANDY SCHUSTER

More defining moments that shpaed the character of Top Business Leaders.

Still, Joe maintains an active role in the business, noting all of the ways that technology has accelerated the pace and scope of what can be accomplished. From struggling to build his business in his backyard garage, the company now has revenues of more than $18 million in annual sales.

With the business on secure footing, Joe is now focusing his customary raw passion for life on the next stage. He spends time with his children and grandchildren, and is looking forward to what the future may hold.

RANDY SCHUSTER

More defining moments that shpaed the character of Top Business Leaders.

MONEY LESSONS

Growing up, Joe learned from his mother about the value of saving and staying out of debt. **"My mother always paid her bills on time, or she would buy on lay-away. Items were paid for before they ever came into the house."** It made a big impression on Joe and his sister and steered Joe away from accumulating debt in his business especially in its early days.

Money to Joe represents freedom and opportunity. Being dependent on others for financing and funding is something to be avoided if possible.

RANDY SCHUSTER

More defining moments that shpaed the character of Top Business Leaders.

138

Mike Mandina

President of Optimax Systems Inc.

---

*"Nothing great was ever accomplished
without hard work and enthusiasm."*

Ralph Waldo Emerson

BUILDING TRUST AND DOING THE RIGHT THING HAVE
BEEN KEY THEMES FOR MIKE MANDINA THROUGHOUT HIS
LIFE, EVEN WHEN LIFE HASN'T GONE AS PLANNED. EARLY
LESSONS IN DISCIPLINE AND PERSONAL ACCOUNTABILITY
GAVE HIM A FRAMEWORK FOR RESTARTING, REBUILDING,
AND ULTIMATELY REJOICING IN HIS SECOND SUCCESSFUL
COMPANY.

It is said that the habits of youth cling to you as you age,
making it important to develop good habits early in life.
When he was just 12 years old, Mike Mandina was already
well into developing the leadership, discipline, and personal
accountability that he would need to be successful as an
entrepreneur. Through his father's role as a scoutmaster,

RANDY SCHUSTER

More defining moments that shpaed the character of Top Business Leaders.

Mike was very involved in the Cub Scouts and Boy Scouts, and as a patrol leader he learned to create schedules, budgets, and action plans with his troop.

Being responsible for others and motivating others was in his blood. His grandfather and father both worked in management positions, and Mike jokes that he really is just a third generation manager. **"At a very young age I didn't expect anybody to plan things or do things for me - I would just be the one doing it."** This ability to self-schedule and manage his time would come in handy during his high school years at McQuaid High School.

Attending the all-male school was Mike's choice, and his parents covered the tuition so that he could go. His freshman year was an adjustment, as very few of his grammar school classmates were attending McQuaid with him. He fell in with a group of wrestlers, who encouraged him to go out for the team. The sport rewarded discipline in training and making weight, while the one-on-one matches encouraged Mike's sense of personal accountability. In his senior year he was a team captain, learning more about leadership and cementing the skill set he would carry forward in life.

From McQuaid, Mike went to St. John Fisher College,

RANDY SCHUSTER

More defining moments that shpaed the character of Top Business Leaders.

majoring in sociology with a minor in psychology. He funded the initial semester with money from his part-time job. Mike had been working as a gas station attendant for his uncle's company since he was 15. He notes that in his family it was understood that, **"If I wanted to have money, I had to go earn it."**

Though not a glamorous gig, the gas station job was a very eye-opening experience. Mike learned the ins and outs of managing a small business, and was very intrigued about the ongoing operational aspects. He also learned about working with the public, and the value of courteous service no matter who he was working with at the time. It was foundational in teaching Mike underlying business concepts.

Back at St. John Fisher, an important question was posed to Mike. His sociology professor had a challenge for the class. "Why are you here?" he asked, pointing out that to make any money or have a serious career in sociology, you needed to be on a path to earning your Ph.D. Reflecting on the question, Mike realized that a Ph.D. wasn't his goal. Fortunately, his roommate at college had a friend in the optics program at Monroe Community College, and after talking with him about the program, Mike thought optics might be a good career choice.

RANDY SCHUSTER

More defining moments that shpaed the character of Top Business Leaders.

Before the start of his second semester, Mike switched from a four year sociology program at Fisher to a two year program in optics at MCC. Since he was paying for his own collegiate education, the cost issue was another factor. Why stay in an expensive program with limited career prospects for non-Ph.D.'s when he could switch to a more affordable program learning practical skills?

At MCC, Mike did just one full-time semester. Then his love for business and working led him to finish school in a part-time program while working for Ilex Optical. At Ilex, Mike worked an overnight shift as a lens grinder before being promoted to a polisher. After a year at the firm he was recognized by the vice president for his talents and promoted into a position as an optics production process engineer.

Unfortunately, Ilex was in financial trouble and would eventually go bankrupt. They would be purchased out of bankruptcy by Melles Groit Inc. It would have been a more traumatic experience had Mike not been approached by an engineer at the firm who asked Mike if he was interested in leaving the company to start a new business venture.

"I had nothing to lose," Mike recalls. He was 23 years old

RANDY SCHUSTER

More defining moments that shpaed the character of Top Business Leaders.

when he helped to found Cormac Industries, a lens design and manufacturing company. From 1976 to 1981, Mike was active in every part of the business, procuring equipment, working contracts and teaching himself how to make optics. The company grew from the initial partnership to 35 employees, and in 1981 they sold the firm to Melles Griot Inc. for a modest sum. Rather than leaving, Mike became the operations manager for the optical systems division.

In 1990, Mike was fired. The business was in a recessionary cycle, and Mike had been ordered to make deep cuts by a new boss. The employees of the company were like his family, many of them people he had personally hired. He refused to make cuts to meet quarterly profit metrics for the parent corporation, and within two weeks he was shown the door. To leave a team and a firm he had helped build from the ground up was a deep emotional blow.

There were financial impacts to deal with as well. Mike's children, now in their early years of high school, and his wife Pat, committed to part time jobs to bring in additional income. While receiving his unemployment and severance, he moved from the part time to the full time MBA program at RIT while he figured out what he wanted to do next. One of the determinations he made during that time frame was that he never wanted to work for anybody like the guy that

RANDY SCHUSTER

More defining moments that shpaed the character of Top Business Leaders.

fired him, and his industry had a lot of people like that, so he would need to work for himself.

Mike started to investigate opening another company. He knew his children were getting ready for college and that he only had a very narrow window of time if he was going to generate enough income to pay college tuition and meet his other financial obligations. It would need to be a pretty aggressive undertaking, and without being independently wealthy, he was going to have to do it on sweat equity and credit cards.

Through a friend, Mike was introduced to the five founding partners of Optimax Systems. They were operating out of a barn basement, and they hired Mike to run the business. The rest of the team had other jobs, so Mike became responsible for the accounting, hiring, process engineering, manufacturing, shipping, packaging, and even cleaning the bathrooms. There was no room for extras in the austere budget of the startup.

The business acquired equipment with credit cards and by trading on Mike's reputation in the industry. From his work with Cormac and Melles Griot, he had a good track record and was trusted, so firms extended the new venture with

RANDY SCHUSTER

More defining moments that shpaed the character of Top Business Leaders.

credit until they had grown enough to qualify for bank loans.

Today, Optimax has more than 150 employees. Many of the original partners have moved on, and Mike shares operational responsibilities with Rich Plympton, whom he met when he hired him at Melles Griot. The firm has moved from the barn basement to becoming one of the Top 100 companies in the Rochester Business Alliance. Mike notes that, **"It's not about the money, it's about the accomplishments."**

MONEY LESSON

Still, it's been quite a transition from the first year, when Mike was only able to take home $7,000. Yet the financial success would not have come without the strength of his reputation. Mike is quick to point out that in order to start a business it takes capital and if you don't have money, all you have is your name and your reputation. **"People don't change that much over time . . . your reputation is everything. Behaving in a responsible and ethical way will pay dividends. Money is just an outcome of doing the right thing."**

RANDY SCHUSTER

More defining moments that shpaed the character of Top Business Leaders.

Chris McVicker

The Flanders Group

---

*"Trust only Movement. Life happens
at the level of events, not of words.
Trust movement."*

Alfred Adler

CHRIS MCVICKER DID NOT HAVE A VISION FOR WHAT HE
WANTED TO ACCOMPLISH WITH HIS LIFE. FOLLOWING HIS
TIME IN THE SERVICE, HE WOULD GO ON TO COLLEGE AND
GRADUATE WITH A BUSINESS DEGREE AND THEN BEGIN A
SUCCESSFUL SALES CAREER IN THE INSURANCE INDUSTRY.
HIS KNOWLEDGE OF THE INDUSTRY COMBINED WITH
HIS DRIVE AND WILLINGNESS TO TAKE RISK IN HIS OWN
BUSINESS WOULD LEAD TO GREAT SUCCESS.

From his childhood home in Baldwinsville, NY, a suburb of
Syracuse, Chris looked out his window and wondered what
he would do when he grew up. He didn't have a specific
career path that he wanted for his future, so when he

RANDY SCHUSTER

More defining moments that shpaed the character of Top Business Leaders.

graduated from high school at 17 he enrolled in a community college to explore his options, before being drafted.

Originally his unit was headed for Vietnam. Chris vividly remembers being at Oakland Air Force Base, preparing for Da Nang, when a need in Germany pulled 50 members of his unit over to Europe instead. Instead of swimming in swamp mud, Chris qualified for the General's football team and spent a considerable amount of time in the service touring Europe. "I was incredibly lucky."

Returning from the service, Chris enrolled at SUNY Geneseo to pursue an undergraduate degree, ultimately graduating from the Jones School of Business in 1972. He still hadn't decided upon a career path, but he was fortunate to have a friend who had gone to work for Liberty Mutual, a property and casualty insurance company, who encouraged him to interview with them to see if they were a good fit.

Liberty Mutual was indeed a good match. In just a few short years, Chris was the eastern division top salesman. He built an impressive book of clients, and because of his success, his love for the insurance industry flourished.

Change was on the horizon. Chris did so well at business development that he was attracting national attention. At

RANDY SCHUSTER

More defining moments that shpaed the character of Top Business Leaders.

25 he was offered the chance at a larger salary and a brand new market to develop.

Chris left Liberty Mutual to run the Rochester Branch of the Nordstrom Agency, an outstanding opportunity for a young sales star. The Agency was acquired by The American Financial Group, and in 1981 they decided to sell the Rochester Branch and offered Chris a lucrative opportunity at a larger branch in Houston, Texas. Both Chris and his pregnant wife, Bernadette, were from upstate New York and didn't want to move out of the area. Yet how could Chris turn his back on this incredible opportunity with a family on the way?

After visiting Houston they returned home and thought things over. Chris had to choose between moving to Houston, changing agencies or going into business for himself. If he were to go out on his own, he didn't want to take existing customers from the company he had worked for. He was uncomfortable with that because of his high level of integrity. Instead, he wanted to figure out a way to finance the purchase of his book of business from The American Financial Group. It was then that an acquaintance called with a proposal that allowed Chris to go into business for himself. He borrowed a nerve-wracking $440,000 to pursue his dream, opening his own insurance

RANDY SCHUSTER

More defining moments that shpaed the character of Top Business Leaders.

business with a partner. The Flanders Group was born on August 27, 1981.

The day was significant in more ways than one. That same day, Bernadette gave birth to their triplet daughters. Chris's stress level went through the roof and many, many sleepless nights followed. He knew how to sell insurance, but he didn't know how to run a business. He had to learn things the hard way.

In his first year of business, Chris had to separate himself from his business partner. He began building The Flanders Group focusing on a team approach. The icon for the business is the Rampant Lion, and the name comes from Flanders, Belgium, the original home of commercial insurance.

In the early years, Chris had to travel all over the state to meet with customers. He was frequently out of town and always stressed out. **"I was waking up in the middle of the night from having thrown up in my sleep,"** he remembers. This was when he could sleep at all. The weight of the debt that he had taken on and the responsibilities of providing for his suddenly large family kept him working hard. His wife, Bernadette, gave up her own career to care for the children and support him, something that he credits with

RANDY SCHUSTER

More defining moments that shpaed the character of Top Business Leaders.

helping him survive the harsh early years as an independent business owner.

After about 10 years of hard work, the company was able to separate itself from the pack by finding its niche, and also by organizing the firm to maximize the profit potential for each employee. **"You're only as strong as your weakest link, so we all worked to ensure that each employee had the potential to grow vertically. I don't want people that need their hands held, and I don't want to be aligning myself with people who lack follow-through."**

The Flanders Group rose to the top one percent of the insurance industry in terms of revenues per employee and profitability as a whole. Yet customer focus is the main drive behind all of Chris's success. He says of insurance, **"It is an industry where you can do a whole lot of good, as long as you put the energy and effort in to make sure that what you're doing is providing a valuable contribution to the customer base."**

Chris notes that networking and relationships were imperative in growing his business. He always looked for referrals from his clients whom he had served well, which opened doors to new customer relationships based on trust.

RANDY SCHUSTER

More defining moments that shpaed the character of Top Business Leaders.

Going forward, Chris plans to continue to focus on the areas of The Flanders Group that he loves. It has been a long time since he has had a sleepless night over the company, wondering if it would be a success. Now he looks back on all of the stress and hard work with a smile, **"You always believe you can do anything when you're young and have that confidence in yourself."**

RANDY SCHUSTER

More defining moments that shpaed the character of Top Business Leaders.

MONEY LESSON

Chris has come to think differently about money as he has moved through life. In the early days of his business, it was hard to get past the struggle of staying in business. He placed pictures on his mirror for the things that he wanted to have or achieve to help him stay motivated as he built the business.

Looking back, he now realizes that money is a tool for creating opportunities. **"When you don't need the money, it puts you in a much stronger position relative to how you react to situations. You don't have to make this deal - you don't have to do anything,"** he says, noting that, having wealth allows you to focus on how you can differentiate yourself and create your vision of what you need to be in business and in life.

RANDY SCHUSTER

More defining moments that shpaed the character of Top Business Leaders.

Tom Merkel

Partner in FM Office Express, Inc.

"Mountaintops inspire leaders, but valleys mature them."

Winston Churchill

HE COULD EASILY HAVE BECOME AN INSTANT SUCCESS BY STEPPING INTO HIS FAMILY'S BUSINESS AFTER COLLEGE, BUT TOM MERKEL CHOSE INSTEAD TO BE INDEPENDENT. DETERMINED TO ENHANCE HIS KNOWLEDGE AND BUSINESS SKILLS BY LEARNING FROM OTHERS, TOM EARNED AN MBA AND WORKED FOR SEVERAL YEARS FOR A NATIONAL ACCOUNTING FIRM AND THEN FOR A FORTUNE 500 COMPANY. ONLY AFTER GAINING THESE EXPERIENCES DID HE FINALLY AGREE TO RETURN TO ROCHESTER AND JOIN THE FAMILY BUSINESS.

Tom Merkel is a Rochester native, growing up in the city's long winters during which he worked a paper route. His father spent Tom's youthful years getting Merkel Donohue

RANDY SCHUSTER

More defining moments that shpaed the character of Top Business Leaders.

going, while his mother stayed at home to keep the family running. Summers were spent in his neighborhood full of kids, and he fondly remembers long hours outside, making his own fun with the group and picking up a love for athletics.

His love for athletics was greater than his love for academics. Sports were Tom's way to be recognized and stand out from his classmates at Brighton High School. He was a member of the football team, a squad that was known for its mediocre performance year after year.

The summer before his senior year, Tom and his teammates decided that this was going to be the year they finally had a great season. They met religiously throughout the summer to practice and run drills together in the spirit of trying to make something happen. None of them were individual stars, and as a team captain, Tom remembers they were runts compared to the teams they played. Their odds weren't good, but they worked hard every day to get prepared and focus on improving. This level of focus was new for Tom, as was the idea of putting aside his personal goals for the good of the team. By the end of the season, after some truly tough games, they emerged undefeated.

Tom carried the lessons of that high school experience with him for the rest of his life. He considers that season and all

RANDY SCHUSTER

More defining moments that shpaed the character of Top Business Leaders.

154

of the work that went into it, to have been one of the most defining times of his life. **"I learned that the person who practices the most will ultimately be the best."**

From Brighton, Tom went on to Ithaca College. He continued playing football and also competed in collegiate track and field events. His goal was to become a physical education teacher, because he loved sports and the physical side of life came easy to him.

Life had other plans. Near the end of his freshman season, Tom suffered a severe leg injury. While he hadn't been fooling himself into thinking he had a professional sports future, his injury meant that he wouldn't be continuing his physical education program.

Tom tried to find something else that would work for him. He tried liberal arts, but didn't like it. He took fine arts, but his teacher informed him that his still life of apples looked like a bowl of bocce balls. He ended up finishing with an accounting degree, a program he found interesting and fairly easy.

"If you get knocked out of something, what got you to where you are isn't necessarily what you will need to get you to

RANDY SCHUSTER

More defining moments that shpaed the character of Top Business Leaders.

155

where you are going." Tom says, "if you can take the skills from what you have learned and apply them to something else, then you will continue to grow." He interviewed for jobs well before he graduated, and found that the lessons he had learned in high school athletics and from his college injury all worked to his advantage.

Though he had initially worried about it, Tom found that interviewing was kind of fun. **"People understood that when you have something in life that is either a hardship or a lesson that you have learned, both can help you to be a good employee,"** he recalls. He accepted a position with what was then one of the Big 8 accounting firms right out of college, and worked for them for the next two and a half years.

Life started pulling him toward New York City, where there was a girl he was particularly fond of - his future wife, Robin. Self assessment had always been a big part of his life, and by looking at what he liked doing and what he didn't, he was able to target a job in finance, taking a position with Nabisco.

The New York City years were good to Tom. He and Robin were married, and he earned his MBA. Nabisco even helped

RANDY SCHUSTER

More defining moments that shpaed the character of Top Business Leaders.

fund his MBA studies at Rutgers, though Tom had to pay a portion of the tuition himself. **"I really learned to study when I had to pay for it, and I learned to appreciate the education I was getting,"** he notes. Tom recalls that he hadn't appreciated his undergraduate education, which his parents had funded, in the same way. He used his skills to take advantage of opportunities at Nabisco, gaining exposure to marketing, sales, and other key operational areas.

One day he got a call from his father, asking him to come home and work in the family business. Twice before, Tom had turned his father down. Now, his father was ready to retire, and serious. "If you don't come home, I'm just going to sell it," he said. Tom was in his early 30s with a successful New York City career, so on one hand there was no reason to stand in the way of a sale. On the other hand . . .

Rochester welcomed Tom back, with Robin by his side. They viewed it as an opportunity to start a family in a good environment, and Tom felt that his time at Nabisco had prepared him for running a business.

It wasn't just any business. Merkel Donohue had been founded by his father, Vic, and his uncle, John Donohue Jr., and it had colored his life growing up. Twelve months

RANDY SCHUSTER

More defining moments that shpaed the character of Top Business Leaders.

157

after coming home, he and two other members of the next generation, John Donohue III and his brother-in-law, John Hedges, bought the business. His father stepped away from the business entirely, leaving them to figure things out in a move that Tom says he has come to respect more and more as time goes by. **"It was one of the best lessons I had because I had to scrape my knees and fix things myself,"** he recalls, although he laughs that it took him nearly 15 years to realize the magnitude of his father's gift to them.

When he was just 42 and his children were six and eight, Tom developed colon cancer. As he went through treatment his whole perspective on life changed. "It was a silver lining, because I'm still here, but it gave me a sense of how to stay connected to my kids and my family."

Tom credits Robin with single-handedly helping pull him through and doing an incredible job of supporting him. He's found that since that time he's accepted the fact that he can't do everything himself, and credits the cancer with helping him to be more patient and to delegate more freely. He is also more considerate in his conversation, reminded that every conversation could be his last and wanting to be remembered well.

RANDY SCHUSTER

More defining moments that shpaed the character of Top Business Leaders.

Today at 58 Tom is in remission, and rarely thinks about his cancer. Instead, he is focused on transitioning out of his business, developing executive coaching opportunities in the community, and supporting his children, Scott and Kelsey, as they launch their own careers. **"If you are willing to continue to persevere through tough situations, you will ultimately get your moment, and if you are prepared for your moment you will be ready."**

MONEY LESSONS

Looking back, Tom remembers that his family didn't start off wealthy. His father was trying to get the business going, and his mother would save by buying boots three sizes too big and stuffing them with newspapers so they could be worn longer as the children grew.

To earn money for himself, Tom had a paper route, and he learned to calculate the value of everything he might want in terms of how many papers needed to be delivered and in what kind of weather. It taught him to appreciate the work that went into earning things. **"Nothing is free, and you don't appreciate something if you don't pay for it."**

With his own family, Tom credits Robin with being a great financial example, and laughs that she may have taught

RANDY SCHUSTER

More defining moments that shpaed the character of Top Business Leaders.

his kids to be too frugal. Yet setting aside savings before spending and always spending less than you make has been central for Tom, and he feels that the idea of competing or keeping up with others is foolish. Instead, by paying yourself first and living within your means, you can achieve comfortable wealth and appreciate what you have.

RANDY SCHUSTER

More defining moments that shpaed the character of Top Business Leaders.

Peter Parts

President of Peter Parts Electronics

"Nothing can add more power to your life than concentrating all your energies on a limited set of targets."

Nido Qubein

PETER PARTS HAS FACED MULTIPLE TURNING POINTS IN HIS LIFE. SOME ARE EASY FOR OTHERS TO UNDERSTAND, SUCH AS HIS BUSINESS CHOICES AND GOAL SETTING MOMENTS. OTHERS HAVE REPRESENTED A UNIQUE CHALLENGE, SUCH AS HIS DIAGNOSIS AT 30 WITH CANCER. THROUGH IT ALL, HE HAS MADE A CONSCIOUS CHOICE TO BE POSITIVE, TO BE FOCUSED AND GOAL-ORIENTED, ALL OF WHICH HAVE GUIDED HIM TO A RICH AND SUCCESSFUL LIFE.

Peter's story begins in Estonia during World War II, where his father fled the invading Russians for the rural fields of South Dakota. The experience taught him that without an education, he would be stuck in the fields his whole life,

RANDY SCHUSTER

More defining moments that shpaed the character of Top Business Leaders.

161

motivating him to earn his doctorate.

When Peter was growing up his father's life lessons were impressed upon him. As a chemist in Dayton, Ohio, his father discouraged sports and pressured Peter to be academically successful. **"You won't have a good life without a good education,"** his father often said, though Peter now counters with a smile that, **"Success has many definitions."**

In college, Peter worked to pay his tuition bills. He took a job with a water softener company in Dayton. It was horribly hard work, lugging 100 pound bags of salt into basements and hauling water exchange tanks around.

A salesperson at the company made two to three times Peter's wages as a laborer, while enjoying shorter hours, company cars, and a well-dressed lifestyle. A high school teacher, Arlene Ackerman, had cultivated Peter's speaking skills, something he'd kept up in his college years. He was confident he had the skills to be a top salesman.

One Friday, a salesman quit. Peter approached his boss and asked to be considered for the vacant sales position. Monday he was fired. His boss felt he had a bad attitude toward the work and told him to go elsewhere if he didn't

RANDY SCHUSTER

More defining moments that shpaed the character of Top Business Leaders.

think salt bag hauling was good enough for him.

It was a strong "no" that was meant to be demoralizing. In response, Peter left and started his own water softener salt delivery service.

Peter remembers that his first day in business he netted just $1.80, enough to buy a quart of milk and a loaf of bread to eat for the day. However, soon he was doing well enough financially to dedicate himself full-time to his business.

Two major turning points were ahead. The first came when a motivational conference would alter his life with its goal setting message. Later, one of his largest clients, Smith Corona, went bankrupt. The experience of working through that on the creditors committee surrounded by financial professionals laid the foundation for Peter's eventual pursuit of an MBA at RIT.

In the meantime, Peter had sold the salt business and took a job in sales at Sears. Naturally a competitor, Peter sought further sales training. He was 23 when he attended a Positive Mental Attitude rally. National motivational speakers like Zig Zigler, Denis Waitley, and Paul Harvey attended, and Peter was most impacted by the importance of goal setting.

RANDY SCHUSTER

More defining moments that shpaed the character of Top Business Leaders.

Peter's mother had always emphasized the importance of attitude and setting goals, but the speakers made those lessons take root. They spoke about the differences in the lives of people who set goals versus those who did not set goals. A Yale study was referenced stating that only 3% of Yale graduates had goals, while 97% didn't. "Today is Friday, and if by Monday you haven't written any goals, then the good news is that you are in the 97% of the majority and you'll be okay. But if by Monday you've written some goals, and you follow them and pay attention to them and read them, then you're going to be in the top 3% of Americans who have goals and if you review them every month you'll be in the top 1%."

Peter slept on that statement. The next day, he went to a nearby park, sat at a picnic table, and created a list of more than 100 things he wanted to do in his life.

The list of dreams and goals became his guidepost for life, and he reviewed them monthly. He still maintains a handwritten goals list and once a year he sits down and reviews his list, adding new goals and noting goals he's completed. Of his original 100 goals, more than 80 have been achieved. Yet the path to achieving those goals has not always been smooth sailing.

RANDY SCHUSTER

More defining moments that shpaed the character of Top Business Leaders.

Five years after his goal setting session, when he was 28, Peter moved to Rochester. The move was prompted by an old friend at a Rochester electronics firm. Seeing a good job opportunity for Peter, he recruited him.

Peter and his wife arrived January 11, 1982. Peter went to work for his friend's firm, and began researching local opportunities to pursue his MBA, which he ultimately earned at RIT. However, a routine physical when he was 30 changed his life dramatically.

It was Peter's first physical, and the doctor found a testicular lump. Peter asked, "Is it cancerous?" His doctor replied, "Don't worry about it, but you should have it looked at."

In the early morning hours two weeks later, Peter sat in a waiting room for his appointment. His doctor looked at the lump and then looked at his watch. "I have an opening at two o'clock today to get you into surgery." Peter was shocked, but his doctor said matter-of-factly, "I've been doing this for 20 years. I've never seen a lump of that size that's not cancer."

Peter was so badly shaken that as he left the clinic that morning he didn't notice the glass exit doors until he walked

RANDY SCHUSTER

More defining moments that shpaed the character of Top Business Leaders.

into them. He'd been given as little as eight weeks to live, though if the removal was successful he might have a long life. Needing more than a few hours to prepare himself, the surgery was scheduled for the next day.

He was lucky, and thanks to surgery and radiation he is now cancer free. Yet the experience changed his perspective. **"To say this is what I want to do with my life, and then have somebody remind you that someday you may only have eight weeks, means that you'd darn well better be working on your goals."** He credits the cancer with helping him to focus on the things that were most important to him.

While all of this was happening in his personal life, his professional life was also changing. After four years working for the firm, he left to start his own business. He was being heavily recruited by other companies, but loved living in Rochester and wanted to capitalize on a gap in his industry - there were no national electronic rep firms.

With his partner Steve Crane, Peter Parts Electronics became the first of its kind. Steve and Peter were a complimentary pair in business, and their early days were humble and hard. Peter and his wife lived on hot dogs and beans, while the tiny warehouse space Steve and Peter shared was so small

RANDY SCHUSTER

More defining moments that shpaed the character of Top Business Leaders.

it had no bathroom (they ordered coffees and small drinks at the local Burger King to access the facilities).

Gradually, the business grew and they could soon afford to put in their own bathroom. By 1996, they moved to a larger location in Rochester, continuing their niche operation of sourcing top quality components and custom items directly from Asia. Now, Peter Parts Electronics is a multinational firm with an office in the Far East, 20 offices in total, 50 independent sales reps, and more than enough bathrooms.

Peter credits his goal setting, focus, and positive attitude with his success. Hard work was also a factor, coupled with the support he received from his work partners and his wife. As for the future, he simply smiles and looks to his goal files. There's plenty to be accomplished.

RANDY SCHUSTER

More defining moments that shpaed the character of Top Business Leaders.

MONEY LESSON

In keeping with his focused and goal-oriented mindset, Peter views money as a tool. **"Money doesn't make you happy, but it gives you a tool that you can use to put to your advantage."** It can have a central role in your life, or it can be a background element. **"I've learned that if I work hard and I work smart, I always end up with enough money to do anything that I've wanted to do,"** which includes many of the 122 items on his life goals list.

Peter has seen many people over the years fall into two camps. He sees those for whom money is really important and there is never enough, and those who have found that they don't need a lot (though "a lot" is a relative term) to have happy and successful lives. He believes that those for whom money is a priority will never be satisfied because there is "never enough", while those who make their families and life goals a priority will be happier.

"When it's all said and done, the important lesson is that people aren't going to say, 'Wow, he was a very successful business man, he made a lot of money.'" Instead, Peter notes that what will be considered is how your time was spent, **"What is important is to use your time well to make the world a better place."**

RANDY SCHUSTER

More defining moments that shpaed the character of Top Business Leaders.

John Place

Mercury Print

"The only thing constant is change."

Francois de la Rochefoucauld

COULD YOU LOSE A MAJORITY OF YOUR BUSINESS OVERNIGHT ... AND STILL THRIVE? JOHN PLACE KNOWS IT'S POSSIBLE. HE HAS NAVIGATED A SEA OF PERPETUAL CHANGE, REINVENTION, AND INNOVATION IN THE PRINTING INDUSTRY THROUGHOUT HIS CAREER. EVEN WHERE OTHERS WOULD HAVE FALTERED OR NOT GIVEN IT THEIR ALL, JOHN DEDICATED HIMSELF TO A BUSINESS HE LOVES AND FOUND THAT SUCCESS LIES IN NEVER STANDING STILL.

In Rochester in the late 1970s, most high school boys chased girls, sports dreams, or a busy social life. John Place didn't do any of those things. Instead, he got up at 5:30 a.m. each day and was at school by 6:00 a.m., finished at noon and headed to work for another eight hours, all of which he

RANDY SCHUSTER

More defining moments that shpaed the character of Top Business Leaders.

chose to do voluntarily.

Entrepreneurship and drive were in his blood. John's mother, Valerie Mannix, ran the precursor to Mercury Print, Mercury Forms, out of the basement of their home on Raven Way. She had seized the opportunity to buy a full set of printing presses and equipment when her former employer went under, setting up shop for herself in 1968.

All through his youth, the print shop was there. Yet John wasn't deeply involved in it. Instead, he worked for Turner Bellows Company as a welder and manager from the time he was a sophomore in high school. The owner, Armand Pontarella, would pick John up from school each day and drop him off after work at home.

Armand served as a friend and mentor to John. **"He really took me under his wing,"** John recalls. He learned about entrepreneurship, the central role of hard work in success, people skills, and business management skills from Armand. By the time he graduated from Gates-Chili High School in 1979, John was managing between 25 and 30 people at the plant, doing work he deeply enjoyed.

Graduation brought a hard choice. Turner Bellows wanted

RANDY SCHUSTER

More defining moments that shpaed the character of Top Business Leaders.

John to work for them, offering an attractive starting salary of nearly $40,000. On the other hand, John's mother, seeing his skills, wanted him to work with her in the printing business, but she only offered $12 an hour. "I had no plans to go to college - I was more of a worker bee than a college person - so I had to make a decision."

In the end, John chose the print shop. "I had to stay with my Mom," he says, noting that Pontarella understood and they remained close friends. Still, Mercury Forms was a very different environment than the manufacturing line. With John joining a small team of just four employees, changes started to happen.

The first thing to change was their basement location. In July of 1979, the company moved to Goodman Street, renting an old house for its business. "It was a cool old house and we became more of a 'real' business," John recalls. His mother made him learn every part of the business, including all the presses and processes, but he spent most of his time with his sales hat on, generating new business.

The business prospered. John had a good working relationship with his mother, and they divided the work to keep things running smoothly. She ran the day to day

RANDY SCHUSTER

More defining moments that shpaed the character of Top Business Leaders.

operations instilling in John the notion that the employees are the most important asset of a company. For his part John sold, relishing the opportunity to get out and open doors. By 1982 they were ready for their own building and bought a location on Magnolia Street to house the additional presses needed in their growing business.

Things flourished for John personally as well as professionally. He married his wife, Mary Beth, and they started their family. As his family grew, so did his company which continued to add employees. They went from four to twenty employees, and changed the name of the business to Mercury Print to reflect the expanding capacity and changing focus of the company.

Together with their largest client, Xerox, the company settled into a pattern of continual evolution. Mercury pushed itself right up to the edge of the latest developments, embracing digital printing and being an early adopter of printing technologies. In 1989 they expanded further and relocated to a building on Adirondack Street.

"Mercury never sits still," says John. All of the change and technology upgrades make the printing business very capital intensive, and the firm constantly had to reinvest

RANDY SCHUSTER

More defining moments that shpaed the character of Top Business Leaders.

in their business model. Fortunately, John's mother had always maintained strong relationships with their banking partners, teaching John the importance of good financial relationships and how those relationships can influence decisions by lenders.

In 1992, they built their own facility at their present location on Holleder Parkway. Running digital print and offset, selling successfully and building strong client relationships had put the business on what appeared to be a smooth path for continued success.

Then came September 11, 2001 ... and John's business nearly went under. The World Trade Centers were a major print location for Xerox, Mercury's largest customer, and the economic shifts following the attacks caused them to pull back on their spending and print projects. "Overnight, the majority of our revenue disappeared," John recalls.

The company had to reinvent itself almost completely, and it wasn't an easy process. They had to make steep cuts, curtailing expenses and laying off staff. "I learned so much, but it was a shock. It was a big turning point for us," John says, noting that the family nature of the company made cutting nearly 25% of the staff extremely painful.

RANDY SCHUSTER

More defining moments that shpaed the character of Top Business Leaders.

The big question was, **"What are we going to do?"** The company had digital print equipment and deep expertise in manufacturing quality print products - they just needed a way to get back to generating revenue. After much thought, John decided to pursue the educational book market.

Together with Christian Schamberger, a rising key employee at the company, John started promoting their educational book capabilities. They rebuilt the business from the ground up one contract at a time, with Mercury's expertise and quality service impressing their new book clients.

The book business grew and presently the company devotes more than 80,000 square feet to book printing and processes. It brings in more business than the core print processes that Mercury was doing prior to September 11, and has been central in keeping the company healthy. **"We opened up a whole new business. We had to reinvent Mercury, and we did,"** John says.

Moving forward, Mercury will continue to innovate, change, and pursue the leading edge of the market. More broadly diversified in his customer base and with his products, John keeps a sharp eye on the future. In 2011, the company will

RANDY SCHUSTER

More defining moments that shpaed the character of Top Business Leaders.

make its biggest capital investment to date with the next wave of printing and ink jet technologies, and John knows this is just the next step. **"The industry is always changing - and we're always transforming ourselves in a different way."** What the future holds may be a mystery, but Mercury and John are ready and waiting to adapt.

RANDY SCHUSTER

More defining moments that shpaed the character of Top Business Leaders.

175

MONEY LESSONS

The key to having money in your pocket is hard work and smart spending. He also counsels a bit of patience with purchases. **"Before you buy anything, think about it for two or three weeks and if you still want it after that time then go out and buy it."** This cuts down on impulsive spending, and ensures that you only buy the things you really want.

Using caution and wisdom with your spending also helps to ensure that you have money available to use as a tool for your business. **"Realistically, if you want to be an entrepreneur, you take risks all day long,"** John says. It's important to balance the risks against the rewards and the capital required, have a good relationship with your bank, develop a good plan, and think of "bumps in the road" as potential opportunities. John notes that in business there will always be risks, but they come with rewards and benefits, too.

RANDY SCHUSTER

More defining moments that shpaed the character of Top Business Leaders.

Ron Reed, MD

Owner of Reed Eye Associates

"If you have the passion, there isn't anything you can't do."

John McTigue

RON REED HAS FACED A NUMBER OF TURNING POINTS IN HIS LIFE, THOUGH PERHAPS NONE SO EXTREME AS HIS EARLY DECISION TO USE EDUCATION TO IMPROVE HIS LIFE. FROM THERE, HE HAS OVERCOME MULTIPLE WOULD-BE HURDLES TO BUILD A SUCCESSFUL BUSINESS AND A LIFE OF MATERIAL COMFORT FOR HIS FAMILY.

"Everyone starts at a different point in life." Ron Reeds starts with this when he tells his story. He was one of two children growing up in a neighborhood on the upper northwestern tip of Manhattan that he says you wouldn't want to walk through - now or then. A move up came when his family was able to get into a low income housing project in the South Bronx. It was a tough life and a tough neighborhood.

RANDY SCHUSTER

More defining moments that shpaed the character of Top Business Leaders.

As Reed looked around, he asked himself an important question that would change his life. "This is my environment, but how do I get out of my environment?" For Reed, education was his exit ticket.

His family was very supportive, and he was the first in his family to go to college. He earned a mathematics degree, but found math too sterile, and decided to pursue medicine.

While his parents supported him emotionally and had put all of their resources into getting him to and through college, it was fortunate that the medical school at the University of Connecticut cost just $600 per year in the early 1970s.

For his residency, Reed chose Strong Memorial Hospital. While he was at Strong, he decided that neurosurgery was too depressing, though he still liked microsurgery. This motivated him to go into ophthalmology. After a year working in General Surgery and the ER at Strong, he left for a residency at Wills Eye Hospital in Philadelphia.

While he was a resident, Reed made $9,000 per year, which was not enough to support his family and two small children. As a result, each Saturday night for three years, he worked an overnight ER shift at the hospital, pairing it with

RANDY SCHUSTER

More defining moments that shpaed the character of Top Business Leaders.

a Wednesday overnight shift at Budd, working as the plant physician from 5:00 p.m. to 8:00 a.m.

Averaging four hours of sleep a day, Reed managed to continue his training. He finished in 1977, and decided to move to an area where he knew people professionally to build a practice. He was 30 when he returned to Rochester.

The move to Rochester was a strategic choice. He could have gone to New York, but felt that it was too hectic and too anonymous to be a good fit for his family and his practice. In Rochester, he felt that he would be able to build a good life and a strong practice because the pace was different and it was possible to build a solid reputation for service in the city.

After a year working with another doctor, Reed launched his own practice when he was just 31. He was fortunate to open the office as his first attempt at financing had failed. The loan officer at Security Trust had looked at his business plan and asked for collateral. Reed replied, "I will collateralize it with my potential." The loan officer said, "We can put no value on that, you're declined."

A second bank made the business loan, allowing Reed to

RANDY SCHUSTER

More defining moments that shpaed the character of Top Business Leaders.

open that July with just himself and his secretary. Business was slow at first after a back-to-school flurry of checkups, prompting his secretary to ask if ophthalmology was a seasonal specialty. Reed replied that he certainly hoped not!

Reed worked part-time in other local hospitals and spread the word with his former associates at Strong that he was available. His work ethic helped him pull in clientele, as did a commitment to never turn anyone away. He remembers receiving calls from people with eye injuries who had called their own doctors and been told, "No, I'm too busy. We'll see you tomorrow." Calling Reed they heard, "You're in pain? Come right over."

Another factor in building his practice was that he never cross-covered the practice. Most practices cross-cover, so that when their office is closed, another practice is covering for them. Reed felt that it depersonalized his practice, and as a result he was on call almost continually for 10 years, something most doctors wouldn't endure.

After a few years, the practice was full, and Reed faced a decision point. He could close the practice to new patients, or he could limit the practice only to surgery. A final option was bringing in additional doctors, a sharp departure from

RANDY SCHUSTER

More defining moments that shpaed the character of Top Business Leaders.

180

standard ophthalmology procedures.

He ultimately chose to become the first practice in Rochester to integrate ophthalmology and optometry. It crossed a traditional turf line and prompted a number of "What are you doing?" calls from his fellow doctors, but Reed felt that both professions had something to offer to his patient population.

Reed also took on traditional operating practices, further setting himself apart. He made his surgeries outpatient operations, following up the next day in his office. Reed received accusations from other ophthalmologists of upsetting the norms and providing sub-standard care, but he stood firm. He felt that instead of a penlight exam in a hospital post-operative bed, he could give better care with a detailed exam in his office with his instruments. Time proved him right, as this methodology is now standard practice nationwide.

Over time, Reed added the third "O" - Optical - to his service package in response to the needs of his patients. He also added a free van service to ensure even older or disabled patients could reach his office. Reed Eye Associates grew to four locations, one surgical center, and 200 employees.

RANDY SCHUSTER

More defining moments that shpaed the character of Top Business Leaders.

A few years ago, residents at Strong asked Reed to share the secret for his phenomenal practice growth. Reed replied, **"I don't have a secret. If your primary goal is to take good quality care of your patients, your practice will grow and grow. If your primary goal is to build a business and not the patient, your practice will die. Your patients don't care what you know unless they know that you care."**

Despite his emphasis on patient care, Reed has been called a businessman who just happens to practice medicine. Reed finds this amusing, noting that when you have a practice like his, everyone you work with depends on you making responsible decisions for their economic well-being.

Even as he achieved success, Reed has found it hard to take his foot off the accelerator. He notes that medicine is a life of delayed gratification, because of all the years of schooling and residency. However he feels fortunate that his hard work has paid off.

"I'm blessed with the fact that I love what I do, which is why I keep doing it. Retirement's not a word in my vocabulary," Reed says, but he has allocated some time to mission work, spending three weeks a year doing surgeries in emerging

RANDY SCHUSTER

More defining moments that shpaed the character of Top Business Leaders.

nations. He feels especially grateful for the opportunity, noting that by taking his children along on the trips, he has been able to teach them values that they otherwise would not have been exposed to.

Reed notes that **"the world does not reward mediocrity, and if you want to be good at anything, you have to put in the same 90 - 100 hours per week that I did. It's not unique to medicine."** Yet he cautions young people looking for their calling, "Don't make the decision based on hours, make the decision based on what you want to do, and then go at it full-tilt." He notes there is fierce competition for today's youth to succeed.

RANDY SCHUSTER

More defining moments that shpaed the character of Top Business Leaders.

MONEY LESSON

Speaking to the youth of today, Reed has the same message that he gives his own children when it comes to money, **"Don't make money your primary focus. Instead, do what you have a passion for, and the success will follow."** To Reed, money is nothing more than an economic scorecard, and it is better to spend the 2,000 to 3,000 hours devoted to working each year doing something you love and enjoy. In this way, you avoid feeling trapped by your work. Still, money does provide a freedom to choose to work or not, which Reed considers to be the ultimate freedom.

RANDY SCHUSTER

More defining moments that shpaed the character of Top Business Leaders.

Bob Relph, Jr.

CEO of Relph Benefits Advisors

"Every adversity, every failure, every heartache carries with it the seed on an equal or greater benefit."

Napoleon Hill

ONE OF THE CONSTANT FORCES IN THE LIFE OF BOB RELPH, JR. HAS BEEN CHANGE. WHILE SOME CLAIM CHANGE IS GOOD, IN BOB'S LIFE THE IMPACT HAS BEEN BOTH POSITIVE AND NEGATIVE. THROUGH IT ALL, HE HAS WORKED TO CREATE SPACES OF SAFETY, SECURITY, AND ULTIMATELY FOUND HIS OWN PATH TO SUCCESS.

The quieter snow belt areas of Rochester, Batavia, Watertown, and Black River were the framework for Bob Relph's youth. He was born in Rochester, but moved to Batavia when he was five. His father worked in the life insurance business, transitioning from Batavia to an office in Watertown when Bob was seven, obtaining a home for

RANDY SCHUSTER

More defining moments that shpaed the character of Top Business Leaders.

185

the family in the nearby village of Black River.

There can be big blizzards and snows in that region. Already a bit unsettled by the change to the Black River schools in mid-year, Bob faced an even more impactful change that next March. The family was involved in a terrible car crash near their home, and his mother was killed. Bob had always been close to her as the only boy in a family of four children and he was utterly devastated. Her death impacted his life forever.

Bob was not alone in struggling after his mother's death. His father also struggled, ultimately remarrying. It was a challenging environment for Bob, as there were now seven children in the family, and they lived frugally with so many people to support. He sought approval anywhere he could find it, sometimes in negative ways. Fortunately, sports became a major outlet, providing him with a place of sanity and safety to replace what was missing in his emotional life since his mother's death.

He started playing football in the seventh and eighth grades. Black River didn't have a team, so his father took the time to make sure he attended practice for the Watertown team each day. He didn't have a very auspicious start as a player, since he was small for his age and his skills needed work.

RANDY SCHUSTER

More defining moments that shpaed the character of Top Business Leaders.

He was actually knocked out by another player in an eighth grade drill, but he refused to give up.

Bob was driven to excel and sports were bringing him back to life. He became the kid on the phone organizing pickup games, and he tied a tire to a tree to throw footballs through, as did Joe Namath when he was young. He had some natural ability, and he put in hours to build his skills so that he could play quarterback. "Sports gave me a sense of confidence, of self-worth and it allowed me to formulate my work ethic. I learned that to excel and be successful demands what not a lot of people are willing to do."

Though he dreamed of quarterbacking and put in hours of practice, Bob still wasn't outstanding. He set himself apart with his effort, and became a starter. However, another change was on its way. In his senior year, the coach switched the team to a wishbone offense, which relied less on throwing and more on the running ability of the quarterback. This was more in line with Bob's natural gifts, and the team went on to the championship that year.

The wishbone offense was not very popular in the Northeast in those days, but it was big with Southern schools. Bob found himself recruited by Colgate, a Division I school, and became the first Relph to graduate from college. He

RANDY SCHUSTER

More defining moments that shpaed the character of Top Business Leaders.

187

started two years as quarterback and had a very successful experience.

In addition to playing football, Bob studied English at Colgate. He liked the historical aspects of literature, and studied writing in order to become an English teacher at the high school level. Immediately after graduation, he accepted a job offer as a head coach and high school English teacher, a job he kept for a year and a half.

In the end, teaching became secondary to coaching, which Bob truly loved. He applied and landed a job as an offensive backfield coach at Davidson College. During his three years there, not only did he enhance his skills, but he met the women's basketball and field hockey coach, his future wife, Dee.

As he turned 27, Bob accepted a position back at Colgate, marrying Dee and taking her with him. They had their first son, Tyler, the next year, and Bob began to rethink his priorities. He loved coaching, but the time commitment was intense. He was working 80 hours a week 10 months a year, coaching football and serving as head coach of the baseball team.

RANDY SCHUSTER

More defining moments that shpaed the character of Top Business Leaders.

Bob notes that a child changes your perspective and he started to wonder if it was time to change his career. His father had always encouraged him to get into the insurance business, but he had never been interested. Now with a family to consider, the opportunities in insurance started to appeal to him.

Circumstances back home were also shifting. His father's early employer and mentor in the insurance business, Tom Maggio, was looking to retire. Maggio had been a guide for his father through his years as a rising star at John Hancock, and even after his father had transitioned to Mutual of Omaha, they stayed in touch. They had become even closer when Bob's father launched his own firm, and Bob's father was in a position now to buy Maggio's book of business so that Tom could retire.

At issue was manpower to run the business. Bob and his father spent long nights walking through the logistics of it all, and Bob talked things over with Dee. Though coaching was the main focus of his life, a change like this could be just what they needed to provide the right balance between work and time with the family.

Now just shy of his 30th birthday, Bob transitioned from football coach to insurance advisor. In his research, he

RANDY SCHUSTER

More defining moments that shpaed the character of Top Business Leaders.

189

discovered Section 125 plans, a cafeteria style benefits program that hadn't yet become available in New York State, though it was popular elsewhere. In 1986, Section 125 plans became his niche to thrive in the local market.

It proved to be a wise choice. From a 600 square foot office and one employee, Bob now has 106 staff members working at his firm. He credits his success to taking the time to find an opportunity. **"Opportunities don't just appear, but if you are searching and constantly open to them, then they come along,"** Bob notes, even though opportunity is often in the form of changes and challenges.

Looking back on his life, Bob continues to be touched by the changes he experienced. He has a careful focus on his family, trying to overcome his own feelings of maternal loss to ensure he expresses his emotions of care and concern to his children. He also maintains the work ethic he developed in football as he grows his business and services his customers, making the long hours count. Now touched with success, he takes time to give back, and looks forward to continuing to make an impact with his work, his family, and his charitable endeavors.

RANDY SCHUSTER

More defining moments that shpaed the character of Top Business Leaders.

MONEY LESSON

Bob credits his father with giving him a great financial foundation and solid business advice. **"Early on he told me that it doesn't matter how much money comes in, it matters how much money you keep, what the profit is,"** something Bob has certainly found to be true. He also values the example of careful money management and frugality that he saw growing up, something he shares with his children even though they never had to live through the powdered milk and other cost control measures he experienced in a family of nine.

He considers his biggest aha moment with money to be the realization that he didn't want to carry any debt and the value of living within his means. Though he wasn't well off at the time, he committed to eliminating all of his debt and operating on a cash only basis based on his true earnings. **"You pay for what you can afford, you don't pay on hope, and you don't make decisions or financial commitments based upon hope for income or revenue."**

Bob views money as a tool for making investments and giving back. In his business, money allows him to hire additional staff and to open new locations, changes he wouldn't be able to make as readily if he had debt. In his personal life,

RANDY SCHUSTER

More defining moments that shpaed the character of Top Business Leaders.

the wealth he has acquired allows him to give back in areas that are important to him, and he looks forward to the chance to see money make a difference to the causes he holds dear.

RANDY SCHUSTER

More defining moments that shpaed the character of Top Business Leaders.

192

Tom Roth

President of Leo J Roth Corporation

"Live a good, honorable life. Then when you get older and think back, you'll be able to enjoy it a second time."

Dalai Lama

TOM ROTH HAS SPENT HIS LIFE WORKING IN THE FAMILY BUSINESS. YET THIS WAS NO CHANCE OCCURRENCE SINCE HIS ENTIRE YOUTH WAS INFLUENCED BY FAMILY BUSINESS VALUES. AS A RESULT, HE HAS LIVED A FULL AND ACTIVE LIFE HERE IN ROCHESTER, BUILDING THE BUSINESS AND BUILDING ON THE RELATIONSHIPS HE HAS BEEN TAUGHT TO APPRECIATE HIS WHOLE LIFE.

Tom's grandfather, Leo J. Roth, started the family business in 1948. Born in 1952, Tom was surrounded by it from the start. Dinnertime conversations were colored by work events, work stories, and work strategies.

RANDY SCHUSTER

More defining moments that shpaed the character of Top Business Leaders.

From his very youngest days, Tom felt that there was an aspect of romanticism about going into the family business. The business was full of history. His grandfather had dropped out of school in the sixth grade to learn a trade, and became a sheet metal worker and roofer. When he started the business, he did it on the strength of his reputation as a hard worker who delivered consistently high quality work.

The business was also driven by Tom's grandfather's fervent passion for the customer. **"We have to be there for them and give them every reason to call us,"** was a lesson that was drilled into Tom's head at a young age.

Along with the dinner table conversations, Tom got his training in the family's way of doing business by spending time at the business. When he was 16 he officially went to work in the shop, sweeping up and helping out on the shop floor where he could.

That first summer when he was 16, as he was walking through the shop on Clifford Avenue, his grandfather came up behind him and told him how happy he was to have him there since he represented the third generation of the family. Not thinking much of the conversation, Tom replied that he, too, was happy to be in the business.

RANDY SCHUSTER

More defining moments that shpaed the character of Top Business Leaders.

However, this seemingly simple exchange didn't end there. "Remember you're a Roth," said his grandfather. "You walk with your head up and a smile, and what part of that don't you understand?"

This comment turned out to be something that really stuck with Tom. He credits it to his grandfather's background, making it important to him that everyone walked with their head high and represented the family and the company well.

Tom treasures his early days at the business and states with pride that Leo Roth Corporation is the only place that he has ever worked. He knows that this makes him unusual, and it surprises many people.

This is not to say that Tom never left the family nest. He went to school at Gannon College which is now Gannon University. Tom got an engineering degree and came home every Christmas break and summer to work in the family business.

He remembers his graduation vividly. Memorial Day, 1974, and the whole family was there to celebrate. His father, Bob Roth, congratulated him on being the first Roth of his generation to graduate. Tom thanked him and let him know

RANDY SCHUSTER

More defining moments that shpaed the character of Top Business Leaders.

195

that he was planning to take a few weeks off between his graduation and starting work. His dad said, "That's what I like about you. We're on the same page. Two weeks off, but on the same page. I'll see you at 7:30 a.m. tomorrow morning." And so Tom went right to work in the shop with no break, starting at 7:30 a.m. the day after his graduation.

With a college degree, he transitioned from the floor to the office. He was paired up with his Uncle Bob Fella, a meticulous man, to learn estimating. It was a proving time for him. Unlike his father and grandfather, he hadn't followed a path through the trades. However, his father had wanted him to go to college and get the business side of things down so that he could manage the company.

Over time, Tom found that his ease with people made sales a natural path for him. This helped him earn respect from the unionized trade workers who had previously dismissed him as a college kid, until they saw that he could bring in new work.

This was his career throughout his 20s. Along with his work life, he had a rich life in Rochester. He traveled with friends, had an active social life, and sailed competitively.

RANDY SCHUSTER

More defining moments that shpaed the character of Top Business Leaders.

In his late 20s, he met his wife, Erin, and Tom credits the marriage as a tipping point in his life. Erin provides him with wonderful companionship and support that he feels is the reason for his ongoing success. Even when work and volunteer commitments pulled him away, Erin was consistently flexible and patient. Her unflagging support despite his many time commitments is something for which he has been continually grateful.

Having joined the Rochester Yacht Club and sailed competitively in his youth, at his father's urging, Tom continued to give a great deal of his time to that organization. He has served as Commodore, one of the youngest ever, which was an honor and point of pride for his family.

He treasures his Yacht Club memories and relationships as additional turning points for him. One key moment came in his youth, when he was just out of college. Henry O'Neill, who docked next to him, asked "How many friends do you have?" Tom replied that he had lots of friends, but Henry pushed back. "Do you know what a friend is? I'll tell you what a friend is. You know someone is a friend, when your car is stranded on the side of the road in Syracuse at 2:00 a.m., you pick up the phone and call them and they say they're on their way. How many of those do you have? You'll

RANDY SCHUSTER

More defining moments that shpaed the character of Top Business Leaders.

know you've had a good life when you have enough friends to carry out the casket."

This was a very thought provoking question for Tom, and a focal point for him. It was after all, a long journey from working on the shop floor to taking over the business, and his friends were important in helping him achieve that goal. Even though it had always been his dream, Tom notes that it's quite a journey between a dream and the execution of the dream.

He credits a great deal of his success to the importance of the friendships and relationships that his father's friend Henry O'Neil reminded him about.

"It's all relationships," says Tom. **"If I was to say one thing to kids, I would say develop relationships and develop friendships."** He feels that many people don't take enough time to make the connections and rich friendships they will need for the rest of their lives.

"I really do believe I am one of the luckiest people in the world. To be able to be in this spot, to have this life - I earned it, but I am very thankful. There are so many things in life that can change it just like that - snap - so I am very, very

RANDY SCHUSTER

More defining moments that shpaed the character of Top Business Leaders.

thankful for what I have because of my father and the other relationships in my life."

MONEY LESSON

"If you do a good job and lead an honorable life, the money will always come," Tom notes. It's a lesson he learned from his father, who also taught him to watch the ways in which he managed his money.

In particular, Tom remembers talking through a large project with his father, debating whether or not to spend a couple hundred bucks here and there for various components of the job. His dad said, "If you saw that money on the road you wouldn't walk by it. If you saw even 50 bucks you'd stop to pick it up, so why are we so casual about giving it away now?"

It was a lesson that not only stuck with Tom, but allowed him to teach others to consider how the smaller elements of a job could add up. Once a worker left about $100 worth of parts and tools on a job site, so Tom picked them up and casually invited him into his office later, leaving $100 lying on the floor. Naturally, the $100 bill was immediately picked up. Tom said, "You picked that up fast, but you left this behind." The worker replied that he'd never thought of

RANDY SCHUSTER

More defining moments that shpaed the character of Top Business Leaders.

it that way, allowing Tom's father's message to become a teachable moment.

Through that message and others like it, Tom both learned and teaches that money is a tool for opportunity. Whether it leads to business expansion, security for the future, or a strong legacy, Tom views money as a commodity that can be used for other, more valuable parts of life. By saving and giving back, he feels it is possible to enrich your life beyond mere financial wealth into an abundance of freedom, success, and the time to spend with those who are most important to you.

RANDY SCHUSTER

More defining moments that shpaed the character of Top Business Leaders.

200

Margaret Sánchez

Principal of Sánchez & Associates

"I must admit that I personally measure success in terms of the contributions an individual makes to her or his fellow human beings."

Margaret Mead

MARGARET SÁNCHEZ EXPERIENCED HER TURNING POINT WHEN SHE WAS STILL IN HIGH SCHOOL. IT CAME FROM AN ENCOUNTER THAT MIGHT HAVE LEFT OTHERS TRAUMATIZED, BUT IT GAVE HER A CONVICTION IN HER PERSONAL IDENTITY THAT SHE WOULD LEVERAGE TO ENJOY A SUCCESSFUL CAREER AS A CONSULTANT AND ULTIMATELY LAUNCH HER OWN BUSINESS.

Margaret grew up in a rural community in the thumb area of Michigan. It was a tiny, agriculturally based town with a population of 1,200, and her extended family was one of the only Mexican American families in the community.

RANDY SCHUSTER

More defining moments that shpaed the character of Top Business Leaders.

Before settling down in Michigan, her parents had been migrant workers. Befriended by the local Presbyterian Church, they made a home for themselves in the community as active volunteers. Since both of her parents worked, her grandmother was the primary caregiver for her and her siblings.

Education was a priority in the household and Margaret was encouraged to dedicate herself to her studies. She also served as a member of her family's financial team as she grew older, helping make financial decisions for the family. That experience left her feeling very capable about handling her own finances, something she has found to be an asset over the years. "If it's about money, you can figure it out," she says.

Yet it wasn't her early financial education that left the most lasting mark. Instead, her biggest turning point came when she was a junior in high school.

Many students in her community took the bus home. Thanks to her father's job as a mechanic, Margaret didn't have to ride the bus, although each day she would walk by the bus on the way to the parking lot. One day, the bus was

RANDY SCHUSTER

More defining moments that shpaed the character of Top Business Leaders.

parked in its usual place, full of elementary school students. As she was walking by with her friends, an elementary boy leaned out the window and called her the n-word.

Margaret wanted to die. She was afraid of her friends' reactions - though they said nothing - and she was absolutely in a state of shock. Ultimately, she continued to her car, shaken to her roots.

However, once in the car, her roots were what came up to support her. Crying because she had been insulted, Margaret realized something she would carry with her for the rest of her life. "I sat in the car and thought, 'I love who I am.' I could have very easily assimilated myself into the dominant white culture, **but that moment reminded me that I truly loved my different identity."** The schoolboy shouting insults became a reminder of who she was, what she loved, and what was important to her.

Even now, remembering that moment makes Margaret emotional. Yet she credits her insulter with being an angel reminding her of everything that she has going for her because of who she is and her family background. From that moment on, she embraced her identity with passion and fervor.

RANDY SCHUSTER

More defining moments that shpaed the character of Top Business Leaders.

When she enrolled at Michigan State University, Margaret was fulfilling the first of many family and personal goals - going to college. Margaret was salutatorian of her high school class and had been saving for college since she was 15 years old.

At college, she dedicated herself to her studies, declaring counseling as a major and intending to work as a high school counselor. She viewed it as a way to make a difference in the lives of students like the one who had insulted her, as well as give back the support she had received from her own high school counselor.

As she studied, she also worked and sent part of her money back to her family to continue to help them. She graduated with a bachelors' degree in liberal arts in 1971, and received her master's degree in 1973.

After graduation, Margaret went to work at a university outside of Detroit. She worked in Special Programs, counseling and working with disadvantaged students in the summers to prepare them for fall enrollment. She came to Rochester in 1982, recruited by RIT to be the Director of College Union & Student Activities.

RANDY SCHUSTER

More defining moments that shpaed the character of Top Business Leaders.

From there, Margaret took a position with the Puerto Rican Youth Development (PRYD), now a part of the Ibero American Action League, the only human services agency that serves primarily Latinos. Her community work led her to other community positions in Rochester until she moved to New York City.

Margaret returned to Rochester when she was 40. It was a unique stage of her life, in that while her professional life was blossoming, her family life was challenging. She had to balance the career she was building in Rochester with a need to support her family in Michigan as her parents and grandmother faced health challenges.

After her mother's unexpected death from cancer, Margaret stepped into a role as the head of her household, driving back and forth from Rochester to her hometown in Michigan on weekends. It was a reprised role that reversed the relationships of her youth. Her grandmother had always been the primary caregiver for the family, but she was now ill and Margaret along with her siblings were caring for the woman she considered her family's life force.

Her grandmother's unconditional love and her insistence that each member of the family could be whatever they

RANDY SCHUSTER

More defining moments that shpaed the character of Top Business Leaders.

wanted to be, was pivotal in Margaret's development. Even growing up in a time when women's roles were changing, and coming from a culture with very strong traditional roles for women, her grandmother both told her and demonstrated that anything was possible for a woman. This made Margaret more comfortable and confident in her career choices in Rochester.

Even as she was facing a tough time in Michigan, her career in Rochester was taking off with a partnership with Walden Hall Associates. It was the first time Margaret had her own firm. The three partners specialized in organizational development work in the community for non-profit groups and human services agencies. They specialized in team building, strategic planning, and diversity.

In 1995, after five years together, the partners separated and Margaret took the opportunity to open Sánchez and Associates. Although she was the sole founder, she now has five junior associates. With the business, she travels all over the country doing diversity and strategic planning work. This covers cultural audits of organizations, training for employees, and determining what is in place, what is not and what recommendations are appropriate to transform the organization into a firm that attracts people from all

RANDY SCHUSTER

More defining moments that shpaed the character of Top Business Leaders.

206

kinds of backgrounds and that makes them feel valued and respected.

Of course, not all of Margaret's life was work. She was and is very active in the community as a result of her upbringing and a feature article that appeared in the Rochester Democrat & Chronicle. The article was a profile of the Puerto Rican Youth Development group that she worked with in the 1980s, and it opened many doors for her on community boards and charitable societies in Rochester over the years.

Each place that she was involved with provided more opportunities to give back. The Red Cross, Rochester General Hospital, Al Sigl Center, and the Community Foundation have all been major parts of her life.

Throughout everything, her experiences and her work have been colored by the experience that she had in high school. **Margaret quotes Eleanor Roosevelt, "In order to really understand and empathize with others, you have to understand who you are and what you're about,"** noting that this is the premise for her life. The choices that she has made as a result of her experience show who she is and how her relationships have influenced her. Though some may have reacted differently, Margaret has built a life around

RANDY SCHUSTER

More defining moments that shpaed the character of Top Business Leaders.

embracing who she really is and what is truly important to her.

When it comes to money, Margaret learned her lessons at a young age due to her family's tough financial situation. She had contrasting examples at home. Her mother's generosity "often left her without two nickels to rub together," while her grandmother, a former migrant with no means of her own, always seemed to have a dollar or two **put aside that she could give to family, especially to her grandchildren when they most needed it. As a result, Margaret learned from her grandmother the value of having something tucked away as savings, and from both her mother and grandmother the importance of giving.**

Now, Margaret thinks about money in terms of three categories. The first is money as a way to fulfill basic needs. The second category is money to support your loved ones. The third is money for philanthropy, which Margaret finds that people tend to associate with giving millions. **"People can be philanthropists in small ways too, even with $5 or $10 donations which become a part of a bigger effort for making a difference in the world,"** she says.

RANDY SCHUSTER

More defining moments that shpaed the character of Top Business Leaders.

Mark Siewert

Past President/CEO Siewert Equipment Company

"What doesn't kill us makes us stronger."

Friedrich Nietzsche

MARK SIEWERT STARTED WITH WHAT HE CALLS "A CHARMED LIFE," BUT THE CHARM PROVIDED NO IMMUNITY FROM MISFORTUNE. WITH THE BIRTH OF HIS FIRST SON, THE DIRECTION OF HIS LIFE WOULD TAKE A SHARP TURN. EVEN THOUGH HAVING A SPECIAL NEEDS CHILD WAS LIFE ALTERING, MARK ACCEPTED THE CHALLENGE AND NOT ONLY HELPED HIS SON BUT MANY OTHERS IN SIMILAR SITUATIONS. MARK'S LEADERSHIP SKILLS AND DETERMINATION HAVE BENEFITTED BOTH HIS BUSINESS AND THE ORGANIZATIONS HE IS INVOLVED WITH.

Early in his life, Mark lived in a world that he found very comfortable. He was the youngest of five, and relates that he had a great family life with wonderful parents and siblings. Living in Brighton, he had good educational opportunities,

RANDY SCHUSTER

More defining moments that shpaed the character of Top Business Leaders.

attending parochial schools including McQuaid Jesuit High School.

He went on to Clarkson University where he did well in an engineering management program. Upon graduation he took a job in Florence, Kentucky succeeding on his own in a sales position with no intention of returning to the family business, Siewert Equipment. However, when he was in his mid-20s, his older brother Jeff called and asked him to come back and help with the business.

After thinking it over, Mark returned to the Rochester area, and went to work for Siewert Equipment. He and his brother decided to buy the business from their father in 1981, the same year that Mark married his wife, Marcia. He was nearly 32, and his life to that point had been what he called "smooth sailing." He had a wife he adored, a solid economic foundation, and a strong family business to grow and manage.

In 1983, Mark Daniel, better known as M. D., was born. Mark's first son had a rare chromosomal abnormality that left him severely mentally and developmentally challenged. The doctors told the Siewert's that their son would never walk or talk, and would live no more than two

RANDY SCHUSTER

More defining moments that shpaed the character of Top Business Leaders.

210

or three years at best.

To call the situation life-changing was something of an understatement. "If this hadn't happened in my life I don't know what I would be, but I would not be the Mark Siewert that I am now, no ifs, ands, or buts about it." Prior to the birth of his son, Mark now realizes that he often took things for granted, thought of himself more than others, and hadn't appreciated his "charmed" life. While having a child is a change for any parent, having a child with special needs was a monumental adjustment for him.

M. D. had health challenges from the start. Looking back, Mark counts himself lucky to have married later in life, so that he had some time to develop the maturity base to handle the situation emotionally, as well as the financial base to handle M. D.'s medical expenses. The first few years after M. D. was born, the family spent significant amounts of time at Strong and Genesee Hospitals, and later developed a relationship with the Mary Cariola Children's Center as they worked on M. D.'s communication skills and physical therapy needs.

The high level of service and care available from the Rochester area hospitals and care centers was an eye-

RANDY SCHUSTER

More defining moments that shpaed the character of Top Business Leaders.

opener for Mark. He experienced firsthand everything that was available to support children and families like his who were facing challenging times. He also built relationships with other parents in similar situations.

A chance encounter led Mark to meet Dan Meyers, who was then on the Board at Mary Cariola Children's Center (Dan soon after became President of Al Sigl Center). As Mark got to know the work and the programs at Mary Cariola better, an idea was born. "I told Dan I would like to join the board at Mary Cariola to see if there was anything I could do."

He could see the needs of other struggling parents, and hoped that he would be able to make a difference. Upon Meyers' recommendation, he became a Mary Cariola board member which proved to be a springboard for further philanthropic involvement.

Each connection and each opportunity led to something else. In addition to the Mary Cariola board, he added a position on the Al Sigl Foundation board and then on the board of Heritage Christian Homes. He built more connections, and branched out from working mainly on fundraising initiatives to taking on more leadership roles.

RANDY SCHUSTER

More defining moments that shpaed the character of Top Business Leaders.

Mark feels that his non-profit work shaped him even as it was helping to shape the lives of others. **"When you are a board chair, you get experiences through other board members. You have experiences other than those of your own. As far as leadership skills go, I probably gained as much through leading non-profit organizations as in leading Siewert Equipment."**

At the time that Mark was increasing his non-profit involvement, his family continued to grow. He and his wife had a second child, Christopher, who did not share his brother's chromosomal abnormality. The family worked to build a balance for both of their sons as they grew, traveling more, taking trips to Disneyworld, and trying to achieve a somewhat normal life.

M. D. defied his doctors in some ways. True to their prognosis, he never did walk or talk, but he could communicate and ultimately lived to be 19 years old.

Mark refers to his son as a challenge but a joy, and finds ways to share happy memories and positive experiences even as he recalls his son's last days. He and his wife spent eight and a half months alternating overnights at Strong Children's Hospital until his son's body finally failed him. The

RANDY SCHUSTER

More defining moments that shpaed the character of Top Business Leaders.

213

experience deepened Mark's commitment to Strong (now named Golisano Children's Hospital at Strong), as his hours there let him witness the many good things that Strong did for children and families.

Looking back, Mark recalls the challenges for his family including his other son, Chris, but also touches on the ways that the experience broadened his perspective and view of the world. Even as his family life centered around the needs of his son in many ways, he was still able to develop a successful business.

Siewert Equipment was founded in 1949 and Mark worked on the sales side for many years. He then focused on management, bringing in his non-profit experiences to help him run the company. He feels he was fortunate to have a business that allowed him to be a hands-on dad, and to have been able to spend so much time in both the for-profit and non-profit worlds.

Naturally, being able to do all of that took careful use of his time. Siewert Equipment was hardly a lifestyle business, and Mark often worked 60 or more hours a week, including Saturdays at the office and often Sundays at home. **"A small business owner is never really off the clock,"** Mark notes,

RANDY SCHUSTER

More defining moments that shpaed the character of Top Business Leaders.

recalling middle of the night planning and thinking about 'what-if' situations for the business even as he dealt with his family situation and his non-profit responsibilities.

Going forward, Mark has left the day-to-day operations of Siewert Equipment behind and spends more time doing his volunteer work along with spending time with his wife and best friend, Marcia and son Christopher. He is excited about the work that he does with the Golisano Children's Hospital at Strong and other organizations.

MONEY LESSON

Throughout his life, Mark has learned that money is the by-product of making the right choices, becoming the right kind of person, and learning the right kinds of things. **"It's a tool that allows you the freedom to live your life how best you see fit, based on the options that you have available."** Mark notes, "You can also use it as a tool to make investments in organizations and causes that are important to you."

Some of the most insightful times that Mark had regarding money came while his son M. D. was in his final long hospital stay. He was reflecting about what he wanted to do with his life, since he was going through a life-changing experience. At the time Mark was reading How Much is Enough? by

RANDY SCHUSTER

More defining moments that shpaed the character of Top Business Leaders.

Pamela York Klainer and more recently he read Peter Buffett's Life is What You Make It. In these books and from his own experiences, Mark identified the core truth that, **"If you earn money on your own, through your own hard work, choices, intelligence, networking, and interactions with others, it's a tremendous source of pride. It helps define your self-worth. On the other hand, when you're gifted money or win the lottery, I don't think you get to appreciate it as you would if you'd earned it."**

RANDY SCHUSTER

More defining moments that shpaed the character of Top Business Leaders.

216

Gary Squires

President of Manning Squires Hennig Co. Inc.

"There is no limit to what can be accomplished if it doesn't matter who gets the credit."

Ralph Waldo Emerson

GARY SQUIRES HAS FACED MULTIPLE TURNING POINTS IN HIS LIFE. HE HAD TO MAKE A LIFE-ALTERING CHOICE AS HE HEADED TO COLLEGE AND LATER FACED AN ILLNESS THAT PUT HIM INTO ANOTHER LINE OF WORK. THROUGH IT ALL, HE HAS VALUED HIS RELATIONSHIPS, MAINTAINED HIS INTEGRITY, AND OVERCOME CHALLENGES TO BECOME A SUCCESSFUL BUSINESS OWNER.

Having grown up in Rochester, Squires has deep roots in the community. His father was a founder of Manning Squires Hennig Company, and from a young age Squires remembers his father's advisors and business partners coming to the house. Working to build his business, his father had a

RANDY SCHUSTER

More defining moments that shpaed the character of Top Business Leaders.

217

bricklayer's eye for details, a reputation for integrity and a commitment to leading by example for his employees and his son.

Squires' business exposure as a child was tempered by his seventh grade teacher, Mrs. Walker. She exposed him to Edgar Allan Poe and taught him to love literature. He credits his teacher for encouraging his life-long love of the arts.

At Byron-Bergen High School, Squires tended to focus on mathematics. This was partially pushed by his parents, who wanted him to study math to take advantage of his own natural abilities. Squires credits Mr. Constantine, his teacher all through his high school years, with giving him the numerical foundation he would leverage the rest of his life.

Yet Squires wasn't all schoolwork and no play. He also participated in high school athletics, learning hard work, character, and the importance of doing the right thing in order to win. Excelling in multiple areas, Squires planned on attending Franklin Pierce University to play soccer and basketball while pursuing a pre-pharmacy degree.

While Squires was completing his senior year, his father

RANDY SCHUSTER

More defining moments that shpaed the character of Top Business Leaders.

218

was making changes at the family business. Richard Manning had died in the 1960s, and by the early 1970s, Squires' father had decided it was time to buy out Richard Hennig. As a result, his parents needed to put all of the family's capital toward the partner buy-out.

Talking things over with his family, Squires had a difficult decision to make. He wanted to go to Franklin Pierce and fulfill his dream of being a collegiate athlete. More than the sports, however, was the educational aspect. Would he have to give up his pre-pharmacy dreams? The family had a difficult decision to make, and Squires ultimately stayed in Rochester and enrolled at MCC.

Looking back, he remembers that during his first semester at MCC, he turned in a rather dismal academic performance. His priorities were elsewhere after he met Catherine, his future wife. Squires jokes that she may not have met an academic all star, but she did meet a damn good dancer!

Still, he pulled himself together to earn better grades in future semesters even as he worked. For extra income throughout his college years, Squires put in hours at his father's firm at night, on the weekends, over the summer, and on school breaks. He did mostly manual work for the firm, picking up industry knowledge.

RANDY SCHUSTER

More defining moments that shpaed the character of Top Business Leaders.

In the meantime, Squires' older brother decided that he was going to pursue a law enforcement career. He became a police officer and later a deputy sheriff. In response, Squires' parents approached him and asked him to leave pharmacy behind permanently to become an accountant so that he could help his father with the business.

Squires thought it over, spending time with his father's accountant to learn more about what that life would be like. In their discussions, Squires could see how being an accountant would allow him to complement his father's business skill set and make a positive contribution to the family firm. It was decided, and so Squires earned an accounting degree from MCC, celebrating his graduation by marrying the love of his life, Catherine. He was 21 years old at the time.

Yet rather than going to work on the books, when Squires graduated he worked with his hands. He was a member of the Local 435, a labor union. For the next few years, he worked in the field with concrete, scaffolding, and building forms. The pay scale was decent, and he counts his co-workers from the Union as some of his greatest friends and allies in life.

Unfortunately, he wasn't meant to work with them forever,

RANDY SCHUSTER

More defining moments that shpaed the character of Top Business Leaders.

however much he enjoyed the job. When he was just 23, Squires contracted a virus that attacked his joints, creating arthritic symptoms and putting him out of commission for nearly a month.

The intense physical work he had been doing would no longer be possible. Forced out of the field, Squires took a position in the company office. His wages as an office worker were half of his previous salary, and he had a learning curve to overcome to do estimates and place materials orders. He also took over some of the firm's accounting, applying what he had learned in school.

Being in the office put Squires in close contact with Eastman Kodak. Manning Squires Hennig Company had done its first project for Kodak in 1978. One of the purchasing agents at Eastman Kodak took Squires under his wing as the companies expanded their relationship. Gradually, he worked more and more as the account manager for the contract and worked to build his overall business management acumen.

He was counseled by Ron Harmon, a long-time loyal member of the firm. Harmon once told him, **"Because your name is Squires, that doesn't give you any flexibility. On the contrary - you have to come earlier, stay later, and work**

RANDY SCHUSTER

More defining moments that shpaed the character of Top Business Leaders.

harder. You have to be the first one up from break and the first one back from lunch because that sets the tone and the example." This was a continuation of his father's work habits, and it stuck with Squires.

He and his father split duties, rather than having Squires spend the day at his father's elbow. Their skills complemented each other, as his father was very detail oriented thanks to his builder's background, while Squires was better at broader estimates. Squires learned to rely on the expertise of others to complement his skills and ensure that there was a good balance between the big picture and the details of each job.

Over time, Squires took on more and more responsibility. Despite the fact that his original goals were in another field entirely, he grew into the role he had chosen. Eventually, he took over from his father and is now the president of Manning Squires Hennig Company. Going forward, he wants to maintain the reputation for hard work, quality, and integrity he inherited and continue to grow the firm. **"I've often said that if I can get through a career in this industry and come out of it with the same reputation that my father had and built for the company, I will have achieved everything."**

RANDY SCHUSTER

More defining moments that shpaed the character of Top Business Leaders.

MONEY LESSON

Squires learned his money lessons from his father. While Squires had a collegiate accounting background, his father had all the books in his head. He always knew where his money was, and he could tell on any given week if he was ahead or behind. For Squires, it was a fundamental point to learn for both his business and personal life, **"You have to know where your money is so you can compare how much is coming in with what you are spending on a regular basis."**

This knowledge builds out into Squires greater perspective on money management. **"It breaks down into two different pieces. There's the making of the money and the spending of the money. If you're spending more than you're making, you have a very short-lived window."** He notes that money should be employed as a tool, and that as you build up capital, try to be conservative and never slide backward. His advice to young people is to live within their means despite the temptations of the world, to set aside at least 10% of their income, and to keep their focus on the truly valuable parts of life.

RANDY SCHUSTER

More defining moments that shpaed the character of Top Business Leaders.

Dan Tessoni

Accounting Professor at the E. Phillip Saunders
College of Business at RIT

---

*"Even if you're on the right track, you'll get
run over if you just sit there."*

Will Rogers

DAN TESSONI HAD TO LEARN HIS LIFE LESSONS EARLY. HE
HAD TO FACE DOWN FINANCIAL HARDSHIP, REJECTION, AND
ROADBLOCKS IN ORDER TO SUCCEED. HIS EDUCATIONAL
ATTAINMENTS, COMMUNITY WORK, AND ABILITY TO BE
CHARITABLE ALL STEM FROM HIS REACTIONS TO THE
TURNING POINTS IN HIS LIFE.

Tessoni grew up in Auburn, NY, the fourth of seven children.
His home life was supportive and warm, although there were
few material luxuries. His mother cared for the children and
worked, while his father held down two jobs, working 3:00
– 11:00 p.m. in a factory and 5:00 a.m. - noon as a milk truck
driver. Tessoni remembers waking up early to ride along to

RANDY SCHUSTER

More defining moments that shpaed the character of Top Business Leaders.

spend time with his father, and the impression his father's work ethic had on him.

The lessons about hard work needed to be put into practice early. Tessoni made the choice to attend a private Catholic High School. Tuition was $20 per month, and there was no way Tessoni could expect his parents to spare that money.

Tessoni worked to earn his own tuition. For four years, he made tuition each month except one. He'd earned the $20 but spent it foolishly. He couldn't borrow from his parents. As a result, he had to go to the school and negotiate more time to pay the bill. He vividly remembers thinking, "I never, ever want to depend on anyone to take care of me again."

Tessoni never missed another payment, and considers the event a major watershed in his life. It made it crystal clear to him that it was his job to take care of himself, a philosophy that has stayed with him ever since.

He was the first person in his family to graduate from high school, and his parents were very proud. His graduation party was a meaningful event for the family enhanced by his commitment to go to college.

The rejection letter in the mail threatened everything.

RANDY SCHUSTER

More defining moments that shpaed the character of Top Business Leaders.

Tessoni had applied to just one school - Georgetown. He was moping around when his father approached him. "Get a grip," his father said. "Just grab the bull by the horns and get on with it. Find somewhere else." The statement had a deep impact, reminding Tessoni not to let one moment of rejection make him give up on his dreams.

Tessoni's "somewhere else" was St. John Fisher College in Rochester, which turned out to be a magnificent experience for him. He majored in accounting, despite previously not really knowing what accounting was or even much about business. He learned, worked, and enjoyed his college years.

Still, he had to work year-round to afford the experience. Summers he slept just three to four hours a night, working two jobs and taking night classes. As a result, he developed an intense work ethic and credits those years with building a positive perception of the role of work in his life. Even now, he tells his students, **"Don't aspire to some great wealth overnight. Earn it - you'll enjoy it more and you'll feel wealthier!"**

When he graduated from Fisher, it was the middle of the Vietnam War and he was facing the draft. To earn a deferment, Tessoni enrolled in Clarkson University for a

RANDY SCHUSTER

More defining moments that shpaed the character of Top Business Leaders.

master's degree in accounting. He shared a house with 10 other students, but was happy to have an assistance ship and his soon-to-be wife, Marty, nearby.

Just before his graduation from Clarkson, the first Vietnam draft lottery was held - the only lottery Tessoni ever won. After graduation, Tessoni shipped out, separating from his wife, and starting a very challenging time. Yet amidst all the darkness, there was the University of Maryland's Far East division, where Tessoni's master's degree enabled him to get a job teaching accounting around his military engagements.

Returning from Vietnam, he took a job with a major accounting firm. His priorities were refocused by his war experience, and he wanted to be sure that he was doing his part to achieve the things that were noteworthy. As a result, two years later he launched his own accounting business.

Initially, he didn't have a deep list of clients. A friend of his wife's working at the National Technical Institute for the Deaf, who knew about Tessoni's master's degree, informed him that they were in desperate need of an accounting teacher. Tessoni had never planned to be a teacher and wasn't sure he was interested, but thought he could at least schedule an interview.

RANDY SCHUSTER

More defining moments that shpaed the character of Top Business Leaders.

It was late spring of 1974 when Tessoni had his interview. It marked his first introduction to the deaf community, and he decided to accept the position. After a 12 week crash course in sign language, Tessoni walked into his first class- 20 deaf students and one hearing person.

He worked very hard with his students, and spent three years teaching accounting in sign language. It was an eye-opening experience, and Tessoni became very involved in the deaf community.

However, all of his involvement made growing his private CPA business a struggle. He debated leaving higher education for the business world, but fate presented him with an opening on the hearing side of RIT's Business School. Making the move, Tessoni became a greater part of the teaching community, and earned tenure as a professor.

His students gave him rave reviews, words Tessoni still holds as more valuable than material wealth. Yet he felt that something was missing, since he was surrounded by Ph.D. but lacked the degree himself. Asking an older professor for advice about whether or not he was a good candidate for a Ph.D., he was told, **"It's 95% work and 5% brains, and**

RANDY SCHUSTER

More defining moments that shpaed the character of Top Business Leaders.

almost everybody has 5% brains."

With the support of the RIT community, Tessoni applied and was admitted to Syracuse University's Ph.D. program. He had been out of school for 10 years when he returned to campus as a student, and found that he really had to work hard to earn the degree. Many times, he debated giving up.

Writing his dissertation was a particular challenge. Tessoni laughingly recalls that he would find almost any excuse to avoid the library. Yet his work ethic and fear of failure kept driving him forward. He told himself, **"If you don't make it, it's not lack of brains. It's that you weren't willing to do the work."**

After seven years of hard work, Tessoni earned his Ph.D. At 39, he found that it afforded him several good opportunities. There were very few Ph.D. in accounting, and Tessoni felt that he was viewed differently as a result.

He kept teaching at RIT, and was invited to participate on various boards in the community, starting with ACC Corporation. Without his educational credentials, he doesn't feel that those opportunities would have ever come his way.

RANDY SCHUSTER

More defining moments that shpaed the character of Top Business Leaders.

"It's a small segment of the world that can get by without credentials, but it is a much, much harder road." After a few years, he discovered a new passion in representing shareholders and business interests as an audit committee member and consultant.

Tessoni has also had the opportunity to be inspired by other leading lights in the community, such as Phil Saunders. The two work together on business development and charitable initiatives, something Tessoni had not envisioned for himself when he was a child.

"I didn't have any money, and I'm not the sharpest tack in the box. I had to work at it, and I needed my degrees to open doors," Tessoni says. Yet after a lifetime of hard work and educational effort, Tessoni is now in a position of success. He looks forward to continuing to teach, continuing his work in the community, and finding a way to continue to help others even after he is gone.

RANDY SCHUSTER

More defining moments that shpaed the character of Top Business Leaders.

MONEY LESSON

From his position now, Tessoni reflects on two main points about finances and wealth generation. The first is an anonymous quote that he heard early in life, **"If you want to help the poor, don't become one of them."** It resonated with him because of his family's background as immigrants from the socialist bloc of Eastern Europe, where their potential was stifled by the environment and culture. In America, there was no stifling, only choices, and Tessoni was reminded of that when he missed his high school tuition payment. Leaving school would put him on a path to nowhere, and he wasn't going to be satisfied with that - he wanted to do well.

This desire for success is his second point in teaching others about money. **"Money follows behavior. Don't signal to the world that you're not capable because you're lazy or not making the effort. It's hard to generate wealth unless you signal to interested parties that you have the ability to do well,"** Tessoni counsels, noting that **"If you've got the skills, if you've got the ability, it's a shame to waste it."** By making the effort to do well in school, in work, and in relationships with others, he feels it is possible to signal that you have what it takes to lead, earn, and participate as a positive force in the community.

RANDY SCHUSTER

More defining moments that shpaed the character of Top Business Leaders.

Peter Webb

Co-owner of Shear Ego Salon & Spa and Shear Ego School

"Very nice Peter, now do it again."

Tom Webb

PERSISTENCE AND DEDICATION HOLD LESS GLAMOUR IN THE PUBLIC MINDSET THAN ROCKETING TO THE TOP, BUT FOR PETER WEBB, IT WAS HIS WILLINGNESS TO PUT IN HIS FULL EFFORT EACH DAY THAT HAS MADE HIM A SUCCESS. FROM HIS FIRST DAYS AS AN APPRENTICE IN HIS FATHER'S SHOP IN ENGLAND TO HIS LIFE AS THE OWNER OF A PRESTIGIOUS HAIR SALON, SPA, AND SCHOOL, FOCUS, HARD-WORK, AND DEDICATION TO HIS CRAFT HAVE ALLOWED HIM TO RISE ABOVE THE REST.

Growing up in Birmingham, England, Peter Webb was surrounded by the hairstyling craft that would later shape his existence. His father operated a successful salon in the King's Heath suburb, while his mother coordinated the

RANDY SCHUSTER

More defining moments that shpaed the character of Top Business Leaders.

books for the business. Peter had an athletic childhood, spending a great deal of his time swimming. His sportive nature gave him a competitive edge that he would always carry with him. In accordance with English tradition, he left school at 15 to become a hairdresser like his father.

Peter had always enjoyed hairdressing, and as he left school he considered it to be a fair trade. Rather than a cosmetology program, the European tradition demanded an apprenticeship. Peter joined his father's salon, honing his skills and entering local and regional stylist competitions.

His first major success came when he was selected as the Best Apprentice of the Year. At 16, he studied for three months in Paris to expand his skills before returning to England and his brisk competition schedule. He won titles in Britain's under-19 stylist division, was European Champion at 18, and was selected to the British World Cup team to do international competitions.

Competing was a joy for Peter, who enjoyed the camaraderie and exposure to the top hairdressers in Europe. Yet each competition carried a price - hours of practice to perfect each skill. He worked from 9:00 a.m. to 6:00 p.m. each day on the salon floor, and then would practice for an

RANDY SCHUSTER

More defining moments that shpaed the character of Top Business Leaders.

additional three to four hours daily. Periodically he would go into London after work for training, returning by train in the wee hours of the morning, only to get up and work another full day.

His father provided him with both creative stimulation and wise counsel. They'd opened a shop in Solihull when Peter was 17 that was one of the first open floor salons in the world, and mixed their own colors, perm solutions, and hair sprays. Still, his father insisted, **"There is no magic. You have to get up every morning, go to work, work all day as best you can, learn as much as you can, and then get up the next day and do the same thing all over again, every day."**

Peter maintained this intensive schedule for more than eight years, competing nationally and internationally. Amsterdam, Berlin, Paris, Barcelona, Geneva, Cologne, and Milan were his playground, working with the original Paul Mitchell and the future British hair magnates Tony & Guy.

In 1961, the World Supreme Hairdressing Competition was hosted in New York. It was Peter's first trip to America, but it would not be his last. He swept the competition to become the World Champion stylist. Along with his title, he picked up a set of friends who hailed from Rochester, NY.

RANDY SCHUSTER

More defining moments that shpaed the character of Top Business Leaders.

Though Peter returned to the business he shared with his father in England, he still kept in touch with his new friends. A discussion on colors and hair pieces led to an invitation from the Rochester Styling Club to come for a teaching visit. While 10 days in Rochester in November might not be an ideal start to a relationship with the city, the area reminded Peter of his native England in certain ways. He deeply enjoyed his trip, and returned via invitation by the styling club to Rochester for the next two years.

While teaching classes as a guest artist at the next New York World Supreme event in 1963, Peter's friends from Rochester planted the seeds for an idea. Why not use his talents to help open a school in Rochester? The idea grew to fruition with the opening of the Peter Webb School in 1965.

The school was a success, and Peter spent many years traveling back and forth, running successful salons on both sides of the Atlantic. Things grew and changed, with expansions and site relocations for his ever growing multinational hairstyling empire. He still made competition appearances as an educator and showcase artist for the love of the craft and the prestige of working with L'Oreal and Goldwell, but the rigorous travel schedule was becoming tiresome and he had his personal life to consider.

RANDY SCHUSTER

More defining moments that shpaed the character of Top Business Leaders.

Peter married at 28 and would have two sons. His father had eased himself out of the business so that it was wholly Peter's by 1980. Though everything was going well, it wasn't perfect, and Peter felt that the oceanic divide in his business life was a part of the problem. Gene Cardmone, a close friend from Peter's first year as a teacher in the States and a decades-long friend in the business, asked, "Why don't you just move to the States?"

He faced a major decision. Would he shut the Rochester shop and keep England, or would he tie up the English side of his operations in favor of America? He had a much larger salon footprint in America and there was the school, but England was his home and an excellent environment for learning and thriving in the hairstylist's trade.

Talking things over with his sons, they came to a temporary solution. One son took over the English salon operations, while Peter, his wife, Shirley, and his other son relocated to Rochester in 1992. **"I've never looked back," he says. "I loved it, still love it today."** Within three years, he convinced his other son to move to America, completely shutting down his English operations.

RANDY SCHUSTER

More defining moments that shpaed the character of Top Business Leaders.

Peter partnered with Gene Cardmone, and now that he resided full-time in Rochester, they continued to expand the concept of the salon and school, working on growing the business. **"You just do it the hard way. You get behind the chair, you do good work, you get personal recommendations, and that is how you build it up."** Having long dreamed of opening a spa, Peter was able to make it happen in Rochester, making it so that his business could do everything related to beauty.

He maintains his international connections, and to this day opens the salon for multi-national training sessions with Goldwell. Peter himself spends two days working the floor and one day in the school each week, keeping up the working tradition that has guided him throughout his long life. He also notes, **"My clients have been very good to me, all through my life,"** reflecting that if you are there for your clients, they will be there for you.

RANDY SCHUSTER

More defining moments that shpaed the character of Top Business Leaders.

MONEY LESSON

Along with a prestigious reputation, Peter has enjoyed financial success. A part of his success comes from the way he was taught to manage his money. Peter's mother taught him to be a saver and a savvy budgeter, pointing out at an early age that there are only 100 cents in a dollar. **"Spend 99 cents of a dollar, and don't go to 101, that's the beginning of the end,"** she said. **"Have a good budget and plan out what you want."** The lessons stuck, as Peter notes that he has always hated owing anyone money, and that he values having a good budget to stick with in his business and personal life.

Still, money was never a primary motivator in Peter's life - it was the craft and the skills-sharing side of the profession. Looking back, he notes that his passion for educating and inspiring others started with his father. He would always say, **"Never be afraid to teach someone else, because if you light another's candle with your candle, it doesn't diminish your flame."** By remaining active in his business and showing an unflagging commitment to teaching quality techniques, it seems that Peter will be lighting flames for many more years to come here in the Rochester area.

RANDY SCHUSTER

More defining moments that shpaed the character of Top Business Leaders.

Christine Whitman

Chairman, CEO, President of Complemar, Inc

"There is only one boss. The customer. And he can fire everybody in the company from the chairman on down simply by spending his money somewhere else."

Sam Walton

YOU CAN EITHER STAND BY AND WATCH SOMEONE ELSE MAKE YOUR FUTURE FOR YOU, OR YOU CAN CREATE YOUR OWN FUTURE. WITH THE RIGHT PERSPECTIVE, CHRISTINE WHITMAN WAS ABLE TO TURN SITUATIONS THAT MIGHT HAVE BEEN FRUSTRATING DEAD ENDS FOR OTHERS INTO OPPORTUNITIES. THESE OPPORTUNITIES HAVE ALLOWED CHRIS TO GIVE BACK TO THE COMMUNITY AND CONTINUALLY UNCOVER NEW PATHS TO FOLLOW.

Growing up, Chris Whitman couldn't have told you what she wanted to do. A native of Fairport, NY, she played a few sports and was a decent student in high school. College was

RANDY SCHUSTER

More defining moments that shpaed the character of Top Business Leaders.

on the horizon for her thanks to the support and insistence of her parents, but as she entered Syracuse University she didn't have any particular goals.

Chris studied a scientific curriculum that included psychology and biology courses, and upon graduation took a job at the University of Rochester (U of R). She served as a lab technician in a research group, still without a specific career direction, but she did gain valuable practical experience to augment her academic background.

From the bright minds around her, Chris learned the scientific method for setting up projects, solving difficult questions, and using data to support her decisions. She credits the U of R with showing her excellence in organizational management and giving her an understanding of how a well-run entity supports the ability of its employees to do good work. These experiences and the knowledge that she gained have served her well throughout her entire career.

The most important thing she learned during her time at the U of R was that she didn't want to spend her life as a researcher. Chris had married in her mid 20s, and her husband Steve's job as a teacher at Brighton High School provided him with an opportunity to chaperone a summer

RANDY SCHUSTER

More defining moments that shpaed the character of Top Business Leaders.

trip to northern Europe. She took a leave of absence from work to go with him and broaden her horizons.

"I loved the notion of traveling and seeing the world," Chris recalls. The trip inspired her to make some changes in her life as a result of her experiences. When she got back from Europe, she was determined to find a new job that would allow her to do more traveling.

The job she took was at CVC as a product manager, which involved traveling the world to visit clients interested in their technology. The company had a strong research-based history in a similar type of technology that she had worked with at the U of R. In 1978, when Chris joined the firm, it had a limited R&D and product development budget.

At 28, Chris was only the second woman manager ever hired by the company. **"I was told that I had to be very careful and to do a great job because it was out of the ordinary to hire a woman for this job,"** she recalls. Yet rather than being intimidated, Chris accepted the challenge and learned a very valuable lesson about meeting client expectations. **"I learned that it doesn't matter what gender or color you are, what type of person you are, whether you have a disability or a perceived one, it doesn't really matter**

RANDY SCHUSTER

More defining moments that shpaed the character of Top Business Leaders.

241

because as long as you are delivering the solution that the client wants they are going to work with you."

As she was learning and honing her skills at bringing products to market for her clients, Chris began to get the sense that CVC was not keeping up with the latest emerging technologies. The current owners were preparing to retire and sell the firm, and were reluctant to invest in more expensive R&D projects. Frustrated, Chris wasn't sure she could stay with the firm.

In her frustration with the decisions at CVC in terms of development projects, Chris opened her eyes to some other offers. She was being pursued by West Coast firms, real movers and shakers with the latest technologies. Yet with two children at home and a husband with a career in Rochester, she didn't want to accept a new job that required her to regularly commute between the coasts. There had to be another way.

Chris decided that she would work to change the company from within and also explore the possibility of eventually purchasing the firm. To prepare, she enrolled in night school, targeting finance and accounting courses. Now the VP of Marketing & Sales at CVC, she traveled the world to meet with clients while juggling her home and family

RANDY SCHUSTER

More defining moments that shpaed the character of Top Business Leaders.

responsibilities. At the same time, she worked with the owners of CVC to prepare the company for the next stage, bringing in partnerships from her research connections at the U of R and obtaining grant funding for new projects.

It was a very taxing time for Chris and her family. She negotiated with the owners to acquire the company for three years. Chris bought CVC in December of 1990 backed by her personal savings and by friendly investors from her distribution network.

"When I joined the company, I had just been looking for a chance to travel and a change," she laughs. Instead, Chris became a massive force for change within the business. It wasn't always easy - all sorts of challenges came along, but the company survived - and thrived.

"Sometimes people think when they become entrepreneurs or go into business for themselves, 'I am not going to have a boss anymore,' and they don't understand we all have a boss - the boss is our customer," Chris states. By developing what her customers really sought, she was able to grow revenues at CVC to ten times what they were when she bought the company. She took the business public, and eventually sold it at a premium to her largest competitor.

RANDY SCHUSTER

More defining moments that shpaed the character of Top Business Leaders.

Bound by a non-compete agreement, some might have simply cooled their heels. Chris returned to Rochester life with a focus on giving back to the community. Together with Larry Peckham, she tackled a frustrating facet of local life: Rochester was a great community with great assets, but other similar communities were doing more to sell themselves and lure new businesses. To address this challenge, they founded Greater Rochester Enterprise (GRE) to woo businesses and create more sustainable job and business opportunities in the Rochester area.

Working with GRE gave Chris the chance to both give back and help strengthen the community she loved. She didn't have to watch other municipalities attract companies that were right for Rochester - she could work to make a difference and seize new opportunities as they emerged. When consultants cited a lack of angel funding for businesses coming to Rochester, she founded the Rochester Angel Network.

Her life as an "angel" also gave Chris the chance to learn about Complemar, the company she currently owns and operates. Complemar was similar to CVC in that it was an established firm with a need for additional R & D and investment in technology. Chris saw an opportunity to

RANDY SCHUSTER

More defining moments that shpaed the character of Top Business Leaders.

reinvent it and since 2004, she has worked to grow the business.

Complemar is just the latest of a lifetime of projects for her, and it's not likely to be her last. Where others might accept things as they are, Chris knows she has the potential to make lasting contributions to her community and her industry. What's next is a page she's waiting to turn.

MONEY LESSON

For Chris, smart money management has presented a lifetime of opportunities. More than anything else, she counsels those just starting out to try and put away a nest egg to cover key expenses. **"One of the reasons that I believe I was willing to take chances in my career is that I always could rely on my ability to pay my bills,"** she says. She and her husband were careful to live on just one income, even though both worked. **"We always had the option to quit our jobs if one of us didn't like what we were doing. I think it helps you be true to yourself and gives you the confidence to go with what you truly believe in."**

In terms of using her present wealth as a tool, Chris's goal is to create jobs in Rochester. **"I have been very fortunate in my career. I have as much as I need, and my expertise**

RANDY SCHUSTER

More defining moments that shpaed the character of Top Business Leaders.

is best served in doing things I'm already good at, which is creating jobs."

RANDY SCHUSTER

More defining moments that shpaed the character of Top Business Leaders.

246

About the Author: Randy Schuster

Turning Points 2 is Randy Schuster's third book. Previous publications have included ***Turning Points*** and ***The Power of Habits: How to be a Rainmaker***. Along with his role as an author, Randy is also one of the nation's leading financial advisors.

Randy views money as a tool that enables him to control his own destiny, manage his time and provide him with financial independence. He had his own aha moment with money when he was young. In his teens and 20s he was always good about saving first, spending second, and not carrying a lot of debt.

Living below his means was a lesson Randy didn't appreciate until he was starting his own business. With discipline about money, perseverance towards his goals, and no debt to hold him back, Randy has been able to launch and control his career as a financial advisor. "Choice is huge," he notes,

RANDY SCHUSTER

More defining moments that shpaed the character of Top Business Leaders.

firm in his belief that if he had been carrying more debt he wouldn't have been able to start a business.

For the last decade he has been ranked in the top one percent of advisors in the nation. He strongly believes that by staying out of debt and committing to a goal, others can find their own pathways to life-long success.

RANDY SCHUSTER

More defining moments that shpaed the character of Top Business Leaders.